Economically Appropriate Technologies for Developing Countries

An Annotated Bibliography

by

Marilyn Carr

Intermediate Technology Development Group

Published by Intermediate Technology Publications
9 King Street, London WC2E 8HN, U.K.

Copyright © 1976 Intermediate Technology Development Group

First published September 1976
2nd impression June 1977

Printed by The Russell Press Ltd, Nottingham, U.K.

ISBN 0 903031 19 1

Contents

Acknowledgement

The publication of this bibliography was made possible by two grants: one, from an anonymous donor, in memory of the Reverend Charles Tett; the other from the Action for World Development Committee of the Episcopal Church of Scotland. Intermediate Technology Development Group gratefully acknowledge their generosity.

Preface

This annotated.bibliography, compiled by Dr Marilyn Carr, will be of great interest and use to individuals and agencies concerned with intermediate technology and the choice of appropriate technologies. There is now a growing awareness of the need to consider these choices within both the rich and poor nations; the widespread, enthusiastic response to *Small is Beautiful* by Dr. E.F. Schumacher is one current indication of this interest. By bringing her fine academic background and practical field experience to bear on this subject, Dr. Carr has produced a timely as well as a practical piece of work.

Shortly before taking up her current position as a Village Technology expert for the UN and ECA in Ethiopia, Dr Carr was commissioned by the Intermediate Technology Development Group (ITDG) to compile these reference materials on the economic aspects of intermediate technology and its appropriateness. While the work of ITDG is now directed towards acting on and answering requests from developing countries for help in locating, developing and initiating appropriate intermediate technical projects, it recognises the continuing need to discuss and demonstrate the economic appropriateness of intermediate technology.

Looking at the Development Decade of the 1960's, Dr Schumacher expressed his concern that "the source and centre of world poverty and underdevelopment lie primarily in the rural areas of poor countries, which are largely by-passed by aid and development as currently practised". (*International Labour Review*, July 1972). In his view, productive employment on an adequate basis was an urgent need, which required that technologies and methods of production must be appropriate to the conditions of poor people in poor countries. They must be cheap enough to be used and maintained by rural and small town populations with low incomes and without sophisticated technical or organisational skills. The technology should draw largely on indigenous resources, and be employed largely to meet local needs. Observing that frequently the labour-saving, capital-intensive technologies of the rich industrialised countries did not meet these conditions — indeed they often aggravated the situation — Dr. Schumacher had, as early as 1962, urged the Planning Commission of India to give high priority to developing and implementing intermediate technologies, especially for rural areas.

By 1966 others from the professions and industry in the UK who shared Dr Schumacher's views joined with him in forming ITDG to bridge the observed gap in development aid: the virtual absence of organised systematic efforts to provide the poor countries with a choice of low-cost, labour-intensive, small-scale technologies, adapted to meet their needs. From the start, ITDG reached two conclusions:- that it was essential to change the emphasis of aid and development programmes towards recognising the needs of poor countries to develop self-help and self-reliance, and:- that much of the basic work of assembling and systematizing knowledge of low-cost technologies could be done in the developed countries.

ITDG therefore set out to compile practical data on intermediate technologies, to test them under operating conditions and to make them widely known and freely available. Beginning with publication of a small guide to relatively simple tools and equipment, which met with enthusiastic interest from developing countries, ITDG has continued to respond to a rising demand from the field for help by coordinating and providing the services of a wide range of intermediate technology field workers and consultants, as well as a journal, *Appropriate Technology,* to facilitate exchange of ideas and information on intermediate technology around the world. Several other annotated bibliographies have been done in the fields of rural health training, low-cost water technologies, and on the Stirling engine.

This bibliography has been compiled in response to the growing number of requests received by ITDG for reference material on the economic aspects of intermediate technology and, in particular, factual information on the economic appropriateness of intermediate technologies for developing countries. The subject is an enormous one and no attempt was made to be fully comprehensive. The fact that only the "hardware" aspects of technology have been covered certainly does not imply that either ITDG or Dr Carr felt that the "software" aspects of technology such as information, education, training, management, and organisation are unimportant. On the contrary, it was felt that they are important enough to warrant a subsequent bibliography in their own right. It is to be hoped that such a bibliography will be compiled in the near future. Further, although the limits of the bibliography have been defined so as to allow as full a survey of the literature as possible, omissions will no doubt be identified, and ITDG would welcome suggestions of relevant publications which could be included in future editions. But even as a "first shot", this bibliography was carefully done and is an excellent job of selection and annotation.

Warren E. Adams,
Professor, Earlham College, and
Economic Consultant, ITDG.

Introduction

The Concept of Appropriate Technology

Perhaps the most important decision facing governments in developing countries is that of technological choice. The question of how existing resources of labour, land, capital and skills can best be combined so as to overcome current problems of unemployment, and provide a stable base for future economic growth, is a complex but crucial one.

It is now agreed that many of the problems currently being experienced in developing countries have been caused, or at least aggravated, by earlier development strategies which stressed the maximization of output through emphasis on large-scale industries, using modern 'Western' technologies. In general, such strategies have not only failed to produce the desired economic growth, but have also contributed to an inability to create full employment and to a rapid rate of migration from rural areas to the already overcrowded cities. This has occured mainly because of an emphasis on capital-intensive techniques, a tendency to locate new industries in a few major cities, and a lack of policy measures aimed at generating productive employment opportunities in rural areas. The problems, along with the social misery and loss of human dignity they involve, are becoming more severe. Any solution must be based on a correction of past trends and, in particular, on the development and dissemination of new types of technology which are more appropriate to the conditions existing in developing countries.

The most immediate need is obviously that of the provision of millions of new workplaces, with the majority being created in the rural areas where 80 to 90 per cent of the population of the developing countries still live. Continued dependence on capital-intensive technologies imported from the West is unlikely to provide more than a fraction of the workplaces needed. On the other hand, traditional techniques, while having a very high labour requirement, are characterized by very low capital and labour productivities and do not generate the surplus needed for rapid growth in capital stock. This has led to the suggestion that what is needed are technologies which are 'intermediate' between these two extremes.

The concept is simple enough. The creation of a workplace at the 'intermediate' technology level would cost £300 as opposed to £3,000 with high technology and £3 with traditional technology. Production is more labour-intensive than when high technology is used and more efficient than if traditional techniques are maintained. Besides being sparing in the use of capital, 'intermediate' technology should also be sparing in the use of skills, should make as much use as possible of local materials, and should cater for local needs such as food, shelter, clothing, water supplies and transportation. Such conditions increase the chances of the technology being successfully integrated into rural communities.

7

The 'intermediate' technologies would appear to hold much greater relevance for the developing countries than do those imported from the West, and the 'intermediate' approach is one which is gaining increasing support. However, criticisms have been made. The most important of these is that 'intermediate' technology is inferior to high-level technology in the sense that it involves lower levels of output for any given amount of capital, and that it creates less surplus and hence restricts the rate of economic growth. Other criticisms are that entrepreneurship is a limited resource and should be concentrated rather than spread thinly over rural areas; that production through 'intermediate' technology involves higher costs and would need protective measures; the quality of output will be lower than if sophisticated technologies are used; and that more use is made of scarce managerial and administrative resources (and especially of supervisory labour) than with less labour-intensive techniques.[1]

An effort has been made in this bibliography to deal with some of these questions in the selection of reference materials. As will be seen in the following section, technological flexibility has been found to exist in many areas of production. Some empirical studies have found that intermediate technology was not the most appropriate one available in the location being considered. This is of course not conclusive, for it generally indicates that better "intermediate" solutions have to be discovered or developed. But the great majority of empirical studies have found that intermediate technology did provide the most appropriate answer under the circumstances. In these cases, the development and availability of an intermediate technology has clearly allowed for a better allocation of resources than would have been possible with existing techniques.

For the reader's convenience, the present guide has been divided into six sections. The first four of these cover technologies related to the basic human needs of food, shelter, everyday manufactured goods (such as clothing, footwear and various household items), and infrastructural goods (such as power sources, water supplies, health services, roads and transportation). The last two sections contain a selection of technical publications and bibliographies which provide useful back-up material to the studies in the main sections.

Although some of the studies, particularly those in the section on power sources, have relevance for developed countries, the majority refer specifically to developing countries. Most of them have been aimed at assessing how 'intermediate' techniques compare in terms of capital and labour productivity, employment generation, cost of production, and generation of surplus with more conventional techniques. It would be unwise to draw any general conclusions from the results of these studies. A technology which is appropriate for one country, or for one area of a country, may not necessarily be the most appropriate under differing conditions prevailing elsewhere. Further, a technology which is the most appropriate for any one area today, will not necessarily be optimal at some future date. However, the studies do raise some important issues, and these have been summarized in an introductory

1. For a summary of these arguments see Schumacher, E.F., *Small is Beautiful* (Blond and Briggs, London, 1973), pp. 152-155; Jenkins, G., *Non-Agricultural Choice of Technique: An Annotated Bibliography of Empirical Studies* (Institute of Commonwealth Studies, Oxford, 1975), introduction by Frances Stewart.

section. They also give some indication as to where gaps in existing knowledge lie. Factual information on technological choice in the production of a whole range of commodities is either negligible or non-existent. Hopefully, the range of products on which research is conducted will widen considerably in the future.

Appropriate Technology in Practice

The empirical studies included in the bibliography raise several important issues. These are summarized here in the, hope that they will add something to the debate on the choice of appropriate technologies and provide some useful guidelines for future research and policy.

For the production of many commodities, a wide range of technically efficient techniques was found to exist. Methods varied from large-scale to small-scale and/ or from very capital-intensive to very labour-intensive. Several studies found that small-scale manufacturing plants were more appropriate than larger ones under existing conditions. (See entries 94, 104, 153, 155.) Factors favouring small-scale production included lower transport costs, reduced demands on management and shorter construction time. Similarly, in agriculture, there is evidence from several countries that small tractors are preferable to large ones, shallow tube-wells are preferable to deeper and more costly ones, and small grain or sugar mills preferable to large processing complexes in terms of unit cost, employment generation, requirements of skills for operation and maintenance, distribution of income, etc. (See entries 21, 32, 40, 48, 49, 52, 59, 75-77.)

In other cases (see entries 118, 120, 121, 123, 124, 139, 141, 152), significant economies of scale were found to exist, although calculations were usually made on the basis of full utilization of large-scale plant and equipment. Owing to limited markets, difficulties in obtaining inputs, frequent breakdowns of sophisticated machinery, power failures, transport bottlenecks, etc., such an assumption is all too often an unrealistic one in developing countries and, in fact, some of the studies go on to show how unit costs either have been or would be increased and returns to capital much reduced at lower levels of utilization. (See entries 61, 121, 123.)

It is often assumed that production at small-scale will be more labour intensive than production at large-scale. Such a link was in fact found to exist in the manufacture of wooden frames (entry 90), and in cement-block making and maize-grinding in Kenya (entries 105 and 73). In each case labour-intensive methods were found preferable at small-scales of production but became inefficient at higher levels of output. On the other hand, a study of various light industries in Indonesia found there was no correlation between scale of output and labour-intensity in any of the industries being analyzed. (See entry 166.)

In situations of mass-unemployment, labour-intensive methods of production obviously have much to commend them. Often, however, a conflict arises in so much as the more labour-intensive techniques involve higher costs than capital-intensive techniques. In such a situation, the choice of technique will obviously depend on what weight is attached to the maximization of employment as opposed to the maximization of future output. Some studies conclude that capital-intensive methods would involve so few employment opportunities in relation to labour intensive alternatives that they should be ruled out, even though they allow for lower costs of production. (See entries 21, 137.)

Several studies found that no conflict arose, with the more labour-intensive methods providing more jobs and, due to low wage rates, having lower costs of production. (See entries 62, 73, 100, 117, 122, 141, 145, 157, 230.) Several others found that although capital-intensive techniques appeared to be preferable when market prices were used, the introduction of shadow pricing to allow for distortions in factor costs would weight the analysis in favour of more labour-intensive methods. (See entries 61, 81, 226, 227.) In some cases (see entry 226), the use of a wage subsidy is recommended as a means of altering the capital/labour ratio in a socially beneficial way. Such measures may encourage some substitution of labour for capital in production, although it is by no means certain that entrepreneurs would choose more labour-intensive techniques, even if these represented the least-cost method of production. For instance, a study of different methods of canning in various countries (entry 117) and a study of various light industries in Indonesia (entry 166) both revealed that, although production costs would be lower with more labour-intensive methods, capital-intensive techniques were being used. Factors responsible for this included brand images allowing firms to hold a monopolistic position in which managers were influenced by non-economic factors, such as ease of management, rather than by price. This has led to recommendations that policies might usefully be aimed at reducing the influence of factors that insulate decision making from local prices and costs.

An interesting point raised by a study of road building in Kenya (entry 225) is that of the danger of concentrating either totally on labour-intensive techniques or totally on capital-intensive techniques. Often a mixed strategy will be the most appropriate, using mechanized techniques for some processes.

Some studies refer to the fact that the choice of product and quality can affect the scale of production and/or the capital/labour ratio. For example, demand for certain maize products necessitates the use of more capital-intensive grinding techniques (entry 73); demand for multi-storey buildings rules out labour-intensive methods of cement block making (entry 105) and labour-intensive building techniques (entry 106); demand for white crystal sugar and white-ware china leads to the use of technologies which are more capital-intensive than those used in the production of traditional sweetening agents or traditional types of pottery (entries 53, 57, 154). A similar point is that a given amount of capital can increase the general well-being of a greater number of people if top quality is not demanded. This is particularly so in the case of road building (entry 224), provision of shelter (entries 103, 107, 108), provision of water supplies and sanitation (entries 201, 203, 207) and health services (entries 212, 213, 218, 219). In such areas, attempts to emulate the standards of the West by providing, for instance, modern hospitals and individual water connections, will simply increase the standard of living of an already wealthy minority while the majority of people in greatest need receive no benefits at all.

Several studies mention the problems involved in deciding between different projects and in measuring costs and benefits of different ways of investing resources. Measurement of benefits appears to have presented the most difficulty in the fields of water supply, sanitation and health (entries 193-195, 198-200, 219). Deciding on which discount rate to use presents further problems. Several studies show how one project (usually that using the more capital-intensive methods) would be preferred at low discount rates, while another would be preferred if a higher discount rate was used (entries 42, 81, 211). One study shows how decisions would differ according to whether choice was based on a cost/benefit ratio, net present worth, or the internal rate of economic return (entry 42). Even if problems of measurement can be overcome, however, and the most appropriate technology decided upon, this does not guarantee that it will be used. In actual decision making, such factors as risk avoidance, appearance of modernity, established procedures and familiar techniques can and do outweigh development policy objectives. (See entries 48, 97, 125, 140).

The studies mentioned so far have dealt with the question of choosing between existing technologies. Several, however, look specifically at technological innovation. Some start from the premise that traditional techniques and materials have a great deal in their favour from the point of view of high labour requirements, ease of operation and maintenance, use of local materials, etc., and show how minor improvements which have overcome cost and quality problems have increased their attraction in relation to modern technologies. This applies for instance to improved animal-drawn equipment (entries 9, 19, 20, 24, 27), improved storage facilities (70), improved village-level mills (52, 75) and improved quality of wood and bamboo for housing (96, 109). Other studies look at attempts to adapt modern technologies so as to make them smaller in scale and/or more labour intensive (entries 57, 94, 104, 115, 154). Generally, the adapted versions have proved to be competitive both in terms of cost and quality with the original versions.

In some cases, innovation has gone beyond the stage of improvement or adaptation of existing technologies and has taken the form of the development of a completely new product or technology which makes optimum use of local labour and materials and meets a previously unsatisfied demand. Examples of this are the indigenous design and development of small tractors (entries 8, 14, 15, 28); the development of various small water-lifting and pumping devices and tube-wells (entries 35, 36, 37, 45, 47); the use of ferro-cement for crop storage, roofing and boat building (entries 66, 82, 86, 89, 98); the development of cookers, drying equipment, etc. utilizing solar energy (164, 167, 173, 178, 187); the development of processes using agricultural and animal wastes to produce methane, animal-feed, building materials, purified water, etc. (85, 168, 170, 181, 182, 196); and the design and development of low-cost vehicles (221, 222). In general these products and processes have been designed to allow for production with a minimum of capital, a minimum of skilled labour and a minimum of imported inputs. This, plus the fact that they were designed to meet a pre-defined need, has, in most cases, led to successful development and dissemination, and to the generation of employment and incomes and savings in foreign exchange.

Only the major issues have been raised here. However, the notes on each entry in the bibliography are fairly comprehensive and readers interested in any particular aspect of appropriate technology, or in a particular commodity, will find numerous minor points of interest in the following pages.

During the course of the research, I benefited considerably from discussions with economists and other experts currently working in the field of appropriate technology. Special thanks are due to Andrew Barnett, Michael Lipton and Len Joy of the Institute of Development Studies; Martin Bell, Gordon MacKerron and Geoff Oldham of the Science Policy Research Unit; Harry Dickinson of Edinburgh University; Eric Clayton and Ian Carruthers of Wye College; Douglas Thornton of Reading University; John Turner of the Architectural Association; and John Boyd, George McRobie and Simon Watt of ITDG. I am also very grateful to Frank Solomon, Editor of Appropriate Technology and Deborah Ainger, Information Officer, ITDG, for passing on the more relevant of the apparently endless stream of articles and books which arrives on their desks.

Intermediate Technology Development Group

Marilyn Carr

Section 1

Agriculture

A. General

1. **Bangladesh Agricultural Research Council,** *Workshop on Appropriate Agricultural Technology* (Dacca, February 1975).

A collection of 19 papers of a fairly general nature on the need for, and the possible areas of application of, appropriate technology in the agricultural sector in Bangladesh. Very few case studies are included, but the collection provides a useful survey of the methodological issues involved in appropriate agricultural technology. Most papers have comprehensive bibliographies.

2. **Child F.C. and Kaneda H.,** *Links to the Green Revolution: A study of small-scale agriculturally related industry in the Pakistan Punjab,* Economic Development and Cultural Change Vol 23 (2) Jan. 1975.

Describes how the small-scale engineering industry in the Punjab responded in the fifties and sixties to the needs of agriculture by supplying tube-well equipment, and setting the stage for the Green Revolution. Development occurred spontaneously without undue resort to loans or other assistance, and few economies of scale have been apparent, with small firms co-existing with larger ones, and producing a competitive product by similar methods. Rising agricultural production has created bottlenecks and imbalances which provide new opportunities for capital formation through backward linkages. There is thus great scope for the development of small-scale threshers, inexpensive reapers, on-farm storage equipment, etc., which could be produced by the indigenous, labour-intensive, small-scale engineering industry. If permitted to interact, the agricultural sector and the small-scale engineering industry would grow in tandem, but the authors suggest that because of current Government policies which emphasize tractors, this process will be aborted.

3. **Duff B.,** *Output, Employment and Mechanization in Philippine Agriculture,* Paper prepared for the Expert Group Panel Meeting on the Effects of Mechanization on Employment, Output and Welfare (F.A.O., Rome, 1975).

Concludes that mechanization in the Philippines has had only a limited effect on both output and employment. However, there appears to be considerable scope for improving agricultural output through mechanization. Irrigation equipment and chemical applicators which improve resource use efficiency, and harvest and post-production innovations which reduce losses and improve quality of output, appear to be promising areas for development and introduction of mechanical technologies.

4.   **Gordon E.,** *Intermediate Technology in West African Agriculture* World Crops Vol XIX (3) 1967.

Argues for the introduction of simple machines into a non-industrial community, where they can improve the indigenous methods and can be regarded as an intermediate stage beween a subsistence economy and an industrial one. The machines can be made locally by the village blacksmith or a village carpenter.

The author mentions the Japanese system of building up relatively sophisticated machinery from components made under contract by numerous individuals equipped with perhaps only one tool suitable for making the one component they specialize in. He suggests that this subcontracting approach could be adopted in West Africa to provide a basic set of agricultural equipment as well as some degree of experience in industrial techniques.

5.   **Green D.A.G.,** *Ethiopia: An Economic Analysis of Technological Change in Four Agricultural Production Systems* (Institute of International Agriculture, Michigan State University, Monograph No.2. 1974).

Analyses four agricultural systems in which technological changes, incorporating appropriate mechanization in the broadest sense of mechanical assistance, are regarded as feasible; and appraises the economic value of proposed technological improvements. Technological changes considered include improved hand-implements, stronger oxen and improved animal-drawn equipment, hired engine-powered equipment, improved storage facilities, and improved pest control and operational efficiency. Reaches the conclusion that relatively unsophisticated technological changes can have a substantial impact on the total development of the economy.

6.   **International Labour Office,** *Mechanization and Employment in Agriculture* (ILO, Geneva, 1973).

A collection of papers surveying the patterns, causes and effects of agricultural mechanization in selected developing countries. Covers Latin America, East Africa, Pakistan, India and Sri Lanka, and the Philippines. Includes much useful empirical data on the output employment and equity effects of substituting tractors and mechanical pumps for animal and/or manpower. General conclusion reached is that the introduction of tractors and mechanical pumps has benefited an already wealthy minority at the expense of society as a whole.

7.   **Khan A.U.,** *Agricultural Mechanization: The Tropical Farmer's Dilemma* World Crops Vol 24 (4) 1972.

Stresses the need for an intermediate mechanization technology to suit the agro-climatic, socio-economic, and industrial conditions of the less developed regions. Argues that the development of such a technology can be accelerated by providing technical assistance to local manufacturers in the form of new machinery designs which can be made easily within the developing countries by low-volume production methods. Cites jeepney manufacture in the Philippines as an example.

Provides some examples of the type of agricultural machinery designs which can help in the establishment of an indigenous farm equipment industry in the developing regions. Machines discussed include a simple row seeder, a lightweight thresher, a portable power-weeder, and a manually operated grain cleaner.

8.   **Khan A.U.** *Appropriate Technologies: Do we transfer, or adapt or develop?* Paper presented at the Ford Foundation Seminar on Technology and Employment (Ford Foundation, New Delhi, March 1973).

Argues that the development of an appropriate technology will require two separate areas of activity: (1) product design; and (2) production engineering. Gives four case studies from Asia which indicate that many modern-sector products can be economically produced in low volume provided product designs and production methods are designed to suit local conditions:-

The IRRI power-tiller: The development and manufacture of a simple 5-7 h.p. power-tiller in the Philippines is given as an example of product development. The design was released by IRRI to two manufacturers in 1972 and by the end of the year they had a combined monthly production of 250 tillers. At the end of 1973, their combined annual production was 3000 tillers, which was three times the number of machines imported into the Philippines in the previous year. At this time, another five companies entered the market and vast increases in production were expected. Work opportunities have been generated in the production of the tillers and in associated marketing and servicing facilities. Also, since the use of tillers has allowed farmers to increase agricultural production, there has been an increase in demand for agricultural workers.

The motor pump: An example of product development in South Vietnam. (See entries 36. Cunningham J.F. and 47. Sanson R.L.)

The Winner engine: A case study of the development of a production process which allows the manufacture of aircooled, gasoline engines (normally high-technology) in low volume, with minimum capital investments. The Thai firm concerned has reduced investment in production equipment by such means as making lathes, grinding machines, etc., in its own small foundry and machine shop. Production has expanded rapidly, and the firm is exporting engines (which are for use in boats) to other Asian countries.

The jeepney industry: An example of product design and innovation in production techniques in the Philippines. (See entry 222. Cabanos P.)

These examples, in which the products are designed to suit available production methods, or in which labour-intensive production methods are developed to permit the manufacture of a complex product, illustrate the kind of engineering inputs that are necessary for the rapid development of appropriate technologies in less developed countries.

9.   **Kline C.K., Green D.A.G., Donahue R.H., and Stout B.A.,** *Agricultural Mechanization in Equatorial Africa* (Michigan State University, Institute of International Agriculture, Research Report No. 6., 1969).

A comprehensive report in which the term "mechanization" is taken to include the use of hand and animal-operated tools and implements, as well as motorized equipment, to reduce human effort, improve time lines and quality of various farm operations, thereby increasing yields, quality of product, and overall efficiency. Part Two contains several case studies of hand-powered, animal-powered and engine-powered agriculture in various parts of Equatorial Africa, and examines the economic and technical aspects of the introduction of improved technology and power into farming systems. Includes numerous examples of simple, low-cost technologies which are appropriate for conditions in Equatorial Africa, and has an extensive bibliography with over 500 entries.

10. **Macpherson G. and Jackson D.,** *Village Technology for Rural Development: Agricultural Innovation in Tanzania* International Labour Review Vol III (2) Feb. 1975.

Points out that intermediate technology, although cheaper than modern mechanized technologies, may still be beyond the reach of many villagers. There is a need, therefore, for even simpler and cheaper technologies, which involve substituting wood for metal as far as possible, and using materials known to and used by villagers e.g. bush poles, planks, nails, scrap iron, leather and rope. Such *village level* technologies would enable villagers, with the help of a simple and inexpensive tool kit and their everyday skills, to construct and keep in working order a whole variety of agricultural implements and equipment. Comparative costs for various implements at the different technological levels are given as follows:-

	Mechanized (list price)*	Intermediate (list price)*	Village level (unit cost)*
Ox-cart/trailer	5,800	710	335
Hand cart		400	150
Cultivator	9,000	192	52
Harrow	7,250	175	60
Wheelbarrow		175	57
Maize sheller		96	53

Tanz. shillings

Also taken into account is the fact that village level technology utilizes village labour between peak cultivation seasons, and thus contributes to rural development generally.

The authors point out that there are cases where IT costs less (per unit of output) and is technically superior to VT; and cases where modern technologies are the most appropriate. VT enables farmers to produce some implements at negligible cost, thus releasing resources for the purchase of intermediate or mechanized equipment in cases where they are the most appropriate. Concludes that a hierarchy of technologies in the correct approach to rural development, and the

VT, a hitherto missing link between hand-powered and intermediate technology, must be given a prominent place in the hierarchy.

11. **Uchanda V.C.,** *The Role of Intermediate Technology in East African Agricultural Development* East African Journal of Rural Development Vol 8 (1&2) 1975.

Examines the role of intermediate technology in the agricultural sectors of East African countries. Mainly theoretical, but includes a few short case studies of appropriate and inappropriate technological change.

12. **United Nations Industrial Development Organization,** *Animal-drawn Equipment, Hand-operated Machines, and Simple Power Equipment in the Least Developed and Other Developing Countries* (UNIDO, New Delhi, Oct. 1974). ID/148 (ID/WG. 193/3).

Explores ways and means to promote the local manufacture of appropriate agricultural machinery in developing countries. Takes a disaggregated approach, and lists projects which would be most suited to individual countries' needs and resources.

13. **Yudelman M., Butler G., and Banerji R.,** *Technological Change in Agriculture and Employment in Developing Countries* (OECD, Development Centre, Paris, 1971).

Chapter Four contains several case studies of the causes and consequences of introducing tractors and engine-powered pumps into various parts of India, Pakistan and Sri Lanka. These show that the introduction of large-scale machinery has resulted in a substantial reduction in the labour requirements within the range of 12 to 27 per cent man-days per hectare. The authors suggest, however, that the paradox of the existence of an abundant supply of agricultural labour in the less developed economies and the adoption of large-scale mechanization need not occur. Selective mechanization may relieve seasonal shortages without unduly displacing labour and thus play an important role in agricultural development.

B. Equipment for Food Production

14. **Aurora G.S., and Morehouse W.,** *Dilemma of Technological Choice: The case of the small tractor* Economic and Political Weekly Vol 7 (31-33) Special number, August 1972.

Discusses the influence of the economic and social climate within India on attempts to develop indigenous technologies. The authors use a specific example of attempts to design and develop a 20 h.p. tractor by way of illustration. Compared to a Czech tractor which would be manufactured under a turn-key arrangement, the indigenous tractor would have been at a disadvantage with respect to cost and initial quality. Since the public sector enterprises are expected, among other things, to make a profit, the tendency was for them to opt for the foreign design, even though the development potential of adopting the indigenous project was greater.

15. **Boschoff W.G.** *Development of the Uganda Small Tractor* World Crops Vol 24 (5) 1972.

Outlines the need to augment human energy on tropical farms, and discusses the merits and demerits of alternative forms of power ranging from animal draught to large-scale tractors. The purpose of developing the Uganda small tractor is indicated as filling a gap in the various alternative power sources. It is emphasized that the tractor is based on local assembly of imported mass-produced components in order to keep the price low. Broad characteristics of the tractor are specified.

16. **Burch D.,** *The Politics of Technological Choice: Agricultural Mechanization in Sri Lanka.* (Science Policy Research Unit, mimeo, 1975).

The paper suggests that the analysis of technological choices cannot be isolated from the differential benefits such choices confer on different social groups. This is demonstrated by an analysis of the political role and power of large farmers, tractor importers, etc., in Sri Lanka which influence the choice of agricultural technology in capital-intensive directions and lead to increased social differentiation.

17. **Carr M.N.,** 'Animals and Tractors in Sri Lanka: A Case Study of Choice of Technique in Agriculture', *Livestock in Less Developed Countries* (Ed). Lipton M. (Frank Cass, London, forthcoming).

Looks at why farmers in Sri Lanka have substituted tractors for draught animals in cultivation, and examines the effects of this process on levels of food production, employment, equity, and quality of rural life. Concludes that subsidies on tractor use played a major part in encouraging the spread of tractorization, and that this had been an inappropriate policy measure in so much as it had encouraged farmers to use a technology which, although privately profitable, was not that which enabled them to achieve maximum levels of food production. Section Four suggests some simple low-cost technologies (e.g. improved animal-drawn equipment, mini-threshing machines, improved storage facilities) which, unlike tractors, could help farmers to increase output, without any undue displacement of labour, worsening income and land distribution, or disruption of rural life.

18. **Deutsch A.E.** *Tractor Dilemma for Developing Countries* World Crops Vol 24 (5) 1972.

Argues that tractors designed for large-scale, sophisticated agriculture are ineffective for small-plot farming. Appropriately sized, simple, low-cost tractors need to be designed specifically to serve emerging agricultural areas. Suitably designed equipment, coupled with careful planning for mechanization, can provide significant gains in the battle for food production. Lists 7 basic design requirements for success in developing countries.

19. **Dima S.A.J. and Amann V.F.** *Small Holder Farm Development through Intermediate Technology* East African Journal of Rural Development Vol 8 (1&2) 1975.

Discusses the reasons for the failure of mechanization policies (based mainly on the introduction of tractors) in East Africa to date, and argues the need for a more appropriate technology. Describes the development of the Kabanyolo tool frames in Uganda which are an improvement on existing ox-drawn equipment. A survey on a sample of farmers who adopted this 'intermediate' technology found that (1) farmers had learnt operation quickly and had expanded acreages of food and cash crops; and (2) 75 per cent of farmers had increased their incomes by 75 to 100 per cent since adoption. Recommends that since intermediate technology has been shown to have a positive effect on peasant farmers income levels, the government should set up local plants to manufacture intermediate technology implements that have been proven suitable.

20. **Gibbon D. et al.,** *Minimum Tillage System for Botswana* World Crops Vol 26 (5) 1974.

Describes the development of the animal-drawn 'Versatool', specifically designed for local conditions and for local manufacture in Botswana.

21. **Hewavitharana B.,** 'Choice of Techniques in Ceylon' *Economic Development in South Asia* (Eds) Robinson E.A.G. and Kidron M. (Macmillan, London, 1970).

Part Six compares alternative techniques for the cultivation of paddy. The characteristics of four alternative methods are as follows:

	A Man with mammoty	B Pair of buffaloes	C Small tractor	D Four-wheel tractor
Hours per acre				
Ploughing	64	16	4 - 6	1½ - 2½
Harrowing	64	4	2 - 3	¼ - 1
Cost per acre (Rs)				
Ploughing	24	19	7	12
Harrowing	24	5	3	5

Concludes that tractors have a cost advantage over traditional techniques, but that they would bring about too sharp a reduction in labour inputs. Concludes that technique B would be the best suited to local conditions. However, there may be some cases in which acute labour shortages make the use of a tractor necessary. In such cases, the small (2-wheel) tractor is to be preferred to the 4-wheel tractor in regard to the cost of production and capital cost. Stresses that while much attention has been given to mechanization, there has been no similar interest in the improvement of simple and indigenous implements using animal power.

The article includes similar analyses of the textile, coir and sugar manufacturing industries.

22. **Hudson J.C., Boycott C.A., and Scott D.A.,** *A New Method of Sugar-Cane Harvesting* World Crops Vol 27 (4) 1975.

Describes a new machine for harvesting sugar-cane, which is thought to be an 'appropriate technology' in the sense of laying stress on the human and technological resources existing in the area of introduction. There are three separate machines: (1) a grab loader; (2) a cane cutter; and (c) a cleaner/bundler. All three are tractor-mounted and can be bought stage by stage, to suit the needs and finances of the individual concerned. Thus, the equipment can be 'plugged in' by stages to match local mechanical skills and any decline in the number of in-field workers available. The entire set of machinery involves a labour input of 1 person for every 20 acres of cane to be harvested. This is 'intermediate' between 1 person for every 5 to 10 acres in the unmechanized state, and 1 person for every 40 to 80 acres with more sophisticated machines.

23. **Inukai I.** *Farm Mechanization, Output and Labour Input: A Case Study in Thailand,* International Labour Review Vol 101 (5) May 1970.

Concludes that since buffaloes could not be used for ploughing before the onset of the monsoon rains (because the soil was too hard), the introduction of tractors had resulted in enormous benefit by enabling ploughing to be done at a time that permitted farmers to change from broadcasting rice to a more labour-intensive transplanting method. This had led to an increase in yields per acre and an increase in labour per acre requirements.

24. **Junion F. and Henry J.** *Can Primitive Farming be Modernized?* (Translated from French by Agra Europe, London).

Chapter Six gives an excellent account, with examples from Africa, of improving existing agricultural tools, introducing new tools, and the role of rural workshops in the maintenance of small tools.

25. **Muckle T.B., Crossley C.P. and Kilgour J.,** *Low Cost Primary Cultivation: A proposed system for developing countries;* (National College of Agricultural Engineering, Occasional Paper No. 1., 1973).

Describes the development of a low-cost power source for land preparation on small (approximately 3 hectare) agricultural holdings in developing countries. The machine consists of 2 parts — a self-propelled winch, powered by a small engine, and a modified ox-tool frame implement which is attached by a cable to the winch unit. Characteristics are: (1) it is designed to allow manufacture in developing countries; (2) it uses local materials as much as possible; (3) it is low-cost — the early 1970's prototype cost approximately £100; (4) it can cope with hard soil (which single-axle and small 2-wheel tractors have difficulty in doing); (5) its performance does not decline with increasing levels of soil moisture (which is a disadvantage with heavy 4-wheel tractors; and (6) it requires 2 operators as opposed to only one in the case of the conventional tractor.

The machine is, therefore, a useful alternative source of draught power to draught animals on the one hand, and existing types of tractor (with all their faults) on the other.

26. Navasero N.C., *Deep Placement Chemical Applicators for Lowland Rice.* (International Rice Research Institute, mimeo, 1975).

Describes two machines for placing fertilizer and chemicals in the root zone of of lowland rice soils. This is found to increase efficiency significantly when compared with surface broadcasting of the chemical in paddy water, and is, therefore, of great value to farmers under conditions of world shortages and rising prices of agro-chemicals.

27. Okai M., *The Development of Ox Cultivation Practices in Uganda* East African Journal of Rural Development Vol 8 (1&2) 1975.

In Uganda, ox-drawn equipment has been developed, and if judiciously applied, can introduce a dynamic process of technical and technological improvements into agriculture. However, support for this 'intermediate' technology has been sporadic. The paper, therefore, aims primarily at stimulating interest in promoting the use of ox-drawn equipment by indicating the potential of the technique in modernizing the agriculture of Uganda. Gives results of a survey showing that the use of oxen results in considerable time-saving over the use of hand tools:

	Primary Ploughing	Secondary Ploughing	Primary Weeding	Secondary Weeding	TOTAL
	(hours per acre)				
Lango hoe	50	46	46	46	188
Ox-implements	11	10	3	3	27

Describes ox-drawn implements in current use, and suggests some improvements that could be made. Concludes that ox-cultivation is better than tractor cultivation, and that the former technique should not be eclipsed by tractorization programmes.

28. Schlie T.W. *Appropriate Technology: Some concepts, some ideas, and some recent experiences in Africa* East African Journal of Rural Development Vol 7 (1&2) 1974.

Attempts to draw together some past 'literature search' work and some recent observations in Africa on the subject of appropriate technology. Includes 2 major case studies:

(1)   The development of an appropriate tractor at the University of Botswana, Lesotho, and Swaziland. The tractor has no gearbox, clutch, differential, belts or chains, and requires no daily maintenance, and has easy manoeuvrability. To go along with the tractor, a programme for the adaptation of hand-controlled ox-implements to utilization by the tractor was begun. Also undertaken has been the development of new equipment for tractor utilization, such as water pumping equipment, irrigation equipment, a circular saw, a corn mill, and an electrical generator. In an attempt to increase efficiency, a unit service exchange scheme was set up, with depots situated at strategic points throughout the country, so that any broken tractor part could be replaced in 12 hours.
(2)   The development of a low-cost tractor at Makere. (See entry 15. Boshoff W.G.)

29. Sen A. *Employment, Technology and Development.* (Clarendon Press, Oxford, 1975). Appendix D: A Study of Tractorization in India.

Surveys the main conclusions of some empirical studies on the impact of tractorization on employment and output. Concentrates on two benefit/cost analyses of tractorization: one in Maharashtra in 1969, and the other in the Ferozepore district in the Punjab in 1973. Concludes that it is so difficult to measure the yield-increasing and cost-saving contributions of tractorization that a 'definitive benefit/cost analysis of this important technological change cannot be done at this stage'.

30. SIET Institute, *Appropriate Technologies for Indian Industry,* (Hyderabad, 1964).

Includes a case study of four techniques for manufacturing a hand-operated Japanese-style paddy weeder. These are: an existing handicraft technique; an existing power-technique; and an improved version of each. In each case, as the table shows, the capital-labour ratio is higher for the improved technique, while the capital-output ratio is lower. The improved versions have lower unit costs than the traditional versions, and the hand techniques have a slightly lower unit cost than the power techniques up to a production level of 2,000 units per month.

	Handicraft Technique (existing)	Power-driven Machinery (existing)	Power-driven Machinery (improved)	Hand-operated Machinery (improved)
Capital equipment (Rs)	150.0	25,000	31,000	7,200
Total employees	1	30	36	32
Production (units/month)	25	850	1,900	1,500
I/O ratio (Rs/units per month)	6.0	29.0	16.0	5.0
I/L ratio (Rs/job)	150.0	835.0	860.0	225.0
Cost per unit (Rs)	14.0	15.0	13.0	12.75

31. Wickramanayake V.E.A., *The Mechanization of Rice Culture in Ceylon,* Journal of the National Agricultural Society of Ceylon Vol 1 1964.

Makes a case for the use of tractors in paddy cultivation so as to increase food production. Looks at the advantages and disadvantages of 4-wheel and 2-wheel tractors. Discusses the Tandem tractor, which consists of two conventional tractors coupled together with the front wheels removed. A Tandem tractor is much cheaper and more efficient than a 4-wheel tractor of similar power. Suggests applying this principle (already popular in many developing countries) to the use of two small (2-wheel) tractors in Ceylon (Sri Lanka).

32. **Wickramanayaka V.E.A.** *The Small Tractor: its use and limitations in the mechanization of Ceylon's agriculture,* Journal of the National Agricultural Society of Ceylon, Vol 2. June 1965.

Compares the work rate and per acre costs of land preparation with hand-tools, animal-drawn equipment, and a small (2-wheel) tractor. Concludes that the small tractor is both the quickest and the cheapest source of draught power for land preparation. The tractor can plough an acre of land in 4 to 6 hours as compared with the 16 hours needed with a pair of buffaloes and 64 hours with hand-tools. Comparative costs of ploughing an acre were found to be Rs. 7.0 with a small tractor as opposed to Rs. 19.0 with buffaloes and Rs. 24.0 with hand-tools.

33. **Wickramanayake V.E.A.** *Evaluation of Agricultural Machinery in Ceylon,* Journal of the National Agricultural Society of Ceylon Vol 5. 1968.

Gives estimates of costs of rotary tilling a paddy field with 5 tractor types:

	4-wheel tractor			2-wheel tractor	
Horse-power	45/50	35/40	20	5/6	6/7
Purchase price (Rs)	23,200	20,700	15,000	3,500	3,800
Work rate (acres/day)	5.0	4.0	3.0	1.5	2.0
Cost per acre (Rs)	31.90	38.90	36.50	15.50	11.50

Finds that while a 4-wheel tractor is much quicker than a 2-wheel tractor, the latter can prepare an acre of land at less than half the cost.

C. Irrigation

34. **Bunyard P.** *Will the Desert Bloom* Ecologist Vol 3 (9) Sept. 1973.

Describes the use of water catchments for agriculture in the Negev, where the average rainfall is only 75 to 100mm per annum. Three different sizes of catchment were tested. These were (a) 350 hectares, which produced only 2.5 mm of run-off with an annual rainfall of 100 mm; (b) 10 hectares, which produced 13 mm of run-off with same rainfall; and (c) 0.1 hectares, which produced 50 mm of run-off. It was also found that for any size of catchment, the run-off increased as the slope decreased. Thus, a slight slope, and a *micro-catchment* gave the best results. Looks at the economics of these schemes. Concludes that even if modern machinery is used for land clearing and making of micro-catchments, the cost is still less than 20 US dollars per hectare. If the work is done by hand, then the cost would be less. If the land to be irrigated was planted under salt-bush, one hectare would produce 30 kilograms of protein, which has a market value of 5 US dollars. Thus, the catchment would pay for itself in approximately 4 years.

35. Clay E.J. *Planners' Preferences and Local Innovation in Tubewell Irrigation Technology in N.E. India.* (Institute of Development Studies, Discussion Paper No. 40., 1974).

A case study of tubewell irrigation in the Kosi area of Bihar, showing how an inappropriate choice of technology led to a misallocation of resources which the agricultural sector was unable to absorb. Explains how it also led to a remarkable series of innovations and adaptations which virtually eliminated the indivisibilities associated with tubewell technology. In particular, a group of farmers experimented with bamboo and coir construction and succeeded in developing a well cased only with bamboo, and a strainer of bamboo and coir. Only 20 to 25 days were needed for construction, and the total cost was only Rs. 100 to Rs. 150. Also, diesel pumping sets were bolted on to bullock carts to provide a mobile source of power for several wells, so overcoming the problem of investment in lumpy capital goods. See also entry 37. Dommen A.J.

36. Cunningham J.F. *The Development of Locally Manufactured Irrigation Pumps in the Republic of Vietnam,* Paper presented at the Second International Seminar on Change in Agriculture, Reading, Sept. 1974.

Until the early 1960's, a suitable mechanical pump at a realistic price was not available in Vietnam, so that the only means of providing supplementary irrigation was by manual water-lifting devices such as water wheels. This meant that only very limited areas were irrigated during the dry season.

This paper describes a major revolution which took place in 1962, when a mechanical pump which could be made locally at low cost was innovated by a delta farmer. Almost all delta farmers possess a sampan boat which is used as the main means of transport, and most families have been able to purchase a small gasoline engine (4-10 h.p.) to power their sampan. The pump innovator discovered that if the sampan propeller was reversed and the driving shaft and propeller were enclosed in a tube of slightly greater diameter than the propeller, the device could pump water up to about 1.5 metres at much greater discharge than the manual devices.

This simple innovation enabled dry season farming to rapidly expand at a marginal cost to the farmer since he already possessed the engine, the driving shaft and propeller. He had only to purchase the pump tube, which in 1973 was marketed for about 5 to 10 US dollars.

See also entry 47. Sanson R.L.

37. Dommen A.J. *The Bamboo Tube Well: A Note on an Example of Indigenous Technology,* Economic Development and Cultural Change Vol 23 (3) April 1975.

A case study of the development of a bamboo tube well by a medium-sized farmer in the Saharsa district of Bihar. The well is made from split bamboo lengths, iron rings and coir string, and its construction is as simple and economical as its sinking into the ground. When a rubber hose is attached to a 5 h.p. diesel pump, and dropped into the open top of the well, water is yielded in quantity. The cost of boring a 60 feet well is Rs. 200 to Rs. 300, which is only 10% of the cost of sinking an iron tube-well to the same depth. Besides being cheap, which means that it is expendable if the well dries up, it can also be made from indigenous or easily available materials. The first well was introduced in January 1969, and by March 1973, there were 33,000 of them in Bihar alone. Loans were available for the sinking of tube-wells so that even the 1½ acre farmer has been able to afford one. The farmer's major investment has now been shifted to the cost of the pumping set, which continues to represent a major hurdle. The cheapest available set in 1973 was Rs. 3,125. The author suggests that a set should be developed costing less than Rs. 1,000.

See also entry 35. Clay E.J.

38. Haque F., *A Comparative Analysis of Small-Scale Irrigation Systems in Bangladesh,* Bangladesh Development Studies, Vol III (1) Jan. 1975.

Uses standard World Bank project appraisal method to evaluate small-scale irrigation projects in Bangladesh. Considers deep tube-wells, shallow tube-wells, and low-lift pumps. Results are shown in the following table:-

	Shallow Tube-well	*Deep Tube-well*	*Low-lift Pump*
Capital requirements (Taka)	6,650	48,000	–
Cost per 100 m^3 of water (Taka)	34	55	47
Percentage of utilization	26	17	13
Benefit/cost ratio (existing capacity)	2.40	1.45	–

Concludes that the deep tube-well, though theoretically more efficient than the shallow tube-well, has not proved so in practice. Unless a dramatic change occurs in the managerial factors which are limiting deep tube-well efficiency, a significant improvement in this technology cannot be expected. In contrast, shallow-tube-well farmers have shown better performance and are expected to do still better if certain facilities (e.g. repair facilities, expert advice and credit) are provided. Recommends that under present socio-economic framework, social gain can further be increased if investment in irrigation is concentrated in shallow tube-wells.

39. Lal D., *Wells and Welfare: An Exploratory Cost-Benefit Study of the Economics of Small-scale Irrigation in Maharashtra.* (Development Centre Studies, Series on Cost-Benefit Analysis, Cast Study No.1, OECD, Paris, 1972.)

Attempts to estimate social costs and benefits to small-scale irrigation from ground water sources, using the OECD Manual Method of Cost-Benefit Analysis. Besides estimating the social rate of return to small-scale irrigation, it also asks whether available irrigation water should be concentrated on a small acreage, or spread more thinly over a wide acreage. It concludes that the latter would be the most appropriate strategy.

40.   Mellor J.W. and Moorti T.V., *A Comparative Study of Costs and Benefits of Irrigation from State and Private Tube-Wells in Uttar Pradesh,* Indian Journal of Agricultural Economics Vol. XXVIII (4) Oct/Dec. 1973.

Compares the economics of private and state-run tube-wells in Uttar Pradesh. Findings are summarized in the following table:

	State tube-well	Private tube-well
Initial investment (Rs)	76,500	5,100
Annual costs (Rs)	18,691	2,282
Cost of water (Rs/1,000 m³)	33	22
Gross returns per hectare (Rs)	910	1,700

Capital costs were (on an annual basis) 7 to 10 times as much for State tube wells as for private tube wells, while the water discharge capacity of the former was only about double that of the latter. Also, the supply of water from state wells was less efficient and less reliable so that those farmers with private wells had a cropping pattern with a greater proportion of high-yielding and cash crops. These farmers were thus able to reap higher profits than farmers using state wells. Factors lowering the efficiency of state wells were: (1) operators were liable to transfer tube-well time to other farms for additional tips; (2) repairs took a long time; (3) wastage of water occurred due to conveyance over long distances; and (4) farms had to forfeit their turn if electricity supplies failed. The authors recommend that less emphasis should be placed on state-tube-wells in the future, and greater concentration placed on the development of private tube-wells.

41.   Mondal R.C. *Farming with a Pitcher: A technique of water conservation* World Crops Vol 26 (2) March/April 1974.

Describes 'pitcher farming' which makes use of baked porous earthern pitchers costing about 0.13 US dollars each. Requires about 800 pitchers per hectare. Water requirements of crops irrigated in this way are only 1.23 to 1.98 cm/ha., which is very small compared to conventional farming systems. This is a useful substitute for techniques such as trickle irrigation, which, although water-saving, require considerable investment and technical skill.

42.   Mukhopadhyay A., *Benefit-Cost Analysis of Alternative Tube-Well Irrigation Projects in Nadia District of West Bengal,* Indian Journal of Agricultural Economics Vol XXVIII (4) Oct/Dec. 1973.

Makes a comparative economic evaluation of deep tube-wells and shallow tube-wells as alternative devices for irrigation. The analysis is done on the basis of 3 alternative discounted measures, namely benefit/cost ratio; net present worth; and the internal rate of economic return. The intention is to gauge whether these 3 different criteria give a different ranking of alternative projects. As can be seen from the table, the deep tube-well would be preferred with the first two of these criteria, but not with the third:

	Benefit/cost (12% discount rate) (ratio)	Net present worth (12% discount rate) (Rs)	Internal rate of economic return (%)
Deep tube-well	2.75	1,253.58	34
Shallow tube-well	1.87	1,245.16	over 50

The author goes on to show that the conclusions vary significantly depending on the discount rate chosen, with the shallow tube-well becoming more attractive at higher discount rates. At a discount rate of 20%, the shallow well would become preferable to the deep well on the net present worth criterion; it would do so at a discount rate of 25% on the benefit/cost criterion. This points out the dangers of assuming and using an incorrect discount rate in evaluations.

Concludes that shallow tube-wells claim a distinct preference over deep tube-wells.

43. **National Academy of Sciences,** *More Water for Arid Lands: Promising Technologies and Research Opportunities* (N.A.S., Washington, 1974).

The report concentrates on little known but promising technologies for the use and conservation of scarce water supplies in arid areas, and aims at drawing the attention of agricultural and community officials and researchers to opportunities for the development of projects with probable high social value. Many of the technologies discussed have immediate local value for small-scale water development and conservation, especially in remote areas with intermittent rainfall.

Topics covered include: rainwater harvesting, run-off agriculture, irrigation with saline water, re-use of water, wells of various types, desalination, rainfall augmentation, iceberg-harvesting, reduction of evaporation, reduction of seepage losses, trickle irrigation, reducing transpiration, and selecting and managing crops more efficiently. The advantages and limitations of each of the technologies are discussed, including questions of cost, skill, environment and local materials. Emphasises new and low-cost developments already made, and points out areas where further research and development is needed. Contains useful bibliographies, and lists individuals and organizations involved in relevant research.

44. **Parker N,** 'A Proposal for a Small-Scale Village Irrigation Programme in S.E. Ghana', *Agriculture in S.E. Ghana Vol. II.* (Eds) Dalton G.E. and Parker N. (Department of Economics and Management, University of Reading, Development Study No.13 June 1973).

Examines alternative systems of promoting irrigation and sets out the economic characteristics of irrigating small-scale farms. Concludes that the small-scale village irrigation project would be economically viable. Such projects would compare favourably with larger more capital-intensive and strictly controlled projects in economic terms, and would have the additional benefit that the existing socio-economic frameworks would be utilized, and there would be a minimum of disruption in the lives of the communities for which the development was being induced.

45. Plessard F., *Etude d'un Système e d'Exhaure á Traction Bovine,* Machinisme Agricole Tropicale. No. 47. Sept. 1974.

Describes a simple animal-powered water lifting device for cattle watering, which was developed at Bambey in Senegal. Tests conducted have given satisfactory results, with the costs of the animal powered unit being 8.5 francs CFA per metre^3 of water, as opposed to 35 to 50 francs CFA for a motor pumped unit.

46. Samuel J., *Development of a Jet Flow Pump.* (International Rice Research Institute, mimeo, 1974).

Propeller pumps and centrifugal pumps are 2 of the most popular mechanically operated pumping devices used in rice production. An inherent limitation of both of these is that their efficiency is considerably affected whenever the operating conditions differ from the optimum. This paper explains how the use of a water jet pump, in combination with a high-head, low capacity centrifugal pump could greatly increase the efficiency of the latter.

47. Sanson R.L. *The Motor Pump: A Case Study of Innovation and Development* Oxford Economic Papers March 1969.

A case study relating how a motor pump developed by local farmers contributed to the development of a major portion of the upper delta region of the Mekong Delta of South Vietnam in the mid-1960's. The pump was adopted rapidly by farmers even though there was no marked Government support, and proved to be extremely profitable. By virtue of allowing extra land to be double cropped it led to a generation of employment opportunities, and eliminated widespread seasonal unemployment.

See also entry 36. Cunningham J.F.

48. Thomas J.W. 'The Choice of Technology for Irrigation Tube-wells in East Pakistan: An analysis of a development policy decision' *Studies if Inappropriate Technologies in Developing Countries* (Eds) Morawetz D. et. al. (Harvard University, Centre for International Affairs, 1974).

Explores in detail the choice of technology for irrigation tube-wells in East Pakistan (Bangladesh). Major findings are shown in the table:

	Low-cost*	Medium-cost*	High-cost*
Initial cost (Rs):			
Market prices	31,660	58,005	194,805
Shadow prices	35,660	94,457	334,727
Internal Rate of Return (%):			
Market prices	48	33	7
Shadow prices	54	25	4

*Low-cost = jet/percussion drilling, centrifugal pump, low speed diesel engine.
*Medium-cost = contractor/power drilling, turbine pump, high speed diesel engine.
*High-cost = contractor/power drilling, turbine pump, electric engine.

On balance, the arguments for the low-cost wells over medium-, and particularly high-cost wells were impressive. East Pakistan's development objectives, economic returns, employment creation and training, the distribution of benefits as well as the potential for the creation of domestic industry would have been better served by the low-cost wells. Ultimately, however, it was the organizational requirements of the implementing agencies, including the aid donors, that determined the choice of technology, and low-cost wells were rejected in favour of medium-cost wells. Thus, in actual decision-making, such factors as risk-avoidance, appearance of modernity, established procedures and familiar techniques outweighed development policy objectives.

49. **Wilkinson R.H. and Kidder E.H.**, 'Irrigation in Developing Countries' *Agricultural Mechanization in Developing Countries* (Eds) Esmay M.L. and Hall C.W. (Shin-Norinsha Co. Ltd., Japan, 1973).

Discusses traditional methods of irrigation and mechanized irrigation methods of varying cost and complexity. Gives comparative costs for 4 types of well in India:

	State Tube-well	Private Tube-well	Persian Wheel	Human Power
	(Rupees)			
Initial investment	76,500	5,100	2,000	1,315
Annual costs	18,691	2,282	727	1,033
Cost of water per 1,000 m^3	33	22	75	120

The private tube-well, which was intermediate between the traditional technologies and the large state tube-well, had the lowest per unit cost.

D. Crop storage and processing

50.   Abbot J.C., et al., *Rice Marketing.* (FAO, Marketing Guide, No. 6., 1972).

Useful section on storage which discusses storage needs (usual error lies in over-estimating requirements); choice between storing rice and paddy; types of storage; storage costs; etc.

51.   Akinrele I.A., *Techno-Economic Feasibility of Small-Scale Distillation of Potable Spirits from Palm Wine,* Paper presented at OECD, Development Centre conference on Low-Cost Technology: An Inquiry into Outstanding Policy Issues, (OECD, Paris, 1975).

Describes the development of a small-scale palm-wine distillation technology in Nigeria. Still in the pilot stage, the plant has an annual production capacity of 25,000 gallons. The total fixed capital investment of one plant is estimated to be 125,000 US dollars, and the probability is estimated at 11.5 per cent of fixed capital. Most of the equipment is operated manually or by batteries; construction costs are kept at a minimum; and by locating the factories in rural and semi-urban areas, the transport costs of palm-wine are kept low.

52.   Arboleda J.R., *Improvement of the Kiskisan Mill.* (International Rice Research Institute, mimeo, 1975).

The 'traditional' kiskisan mill is widely used for milling rice in Asian countries, but as it is characterized by a low milling recovery (60 to 63 per cent as opposed to 70 per cent for a modern mill), and high grain breakage, governments have tended to discourage further use and installation, and to encourage the installation of large modern mills which require large capital investments. There are, however, numerous advantages attached to the kiskisan mill, including its low initial and maintenance cost, its simplicity of construction and operation, its capability of being locally produced, its ability to mill small quantities of rice, and the possibility of using the by-product of ground husk-bran mixture as feed for backyard-raised animals. This paper describes how improvements can be made to the 'village-level' kiskisan mill to help prevent grain loss, so that the argument for retaining it is strengthened.

53.   Baron C.G., 'Sugar Processing Techniques in India' *Technology and Employment in Industry* (Ed) Bhalla A.S. (ILO, Geneva, 1975).

Compares a small-scale intermediate technology for making white sugar, and a larger and better established capital-intensive production process. The choice between the 2 technologies is analyzed with reference both to private profitability and to the social costs of production, drawing upon the considerations on shadow pricing in the surplus labour economy suggested in several works, most notably in the UNIDO Guidelines for Project Evaluation. The over-all conclusion tends to bear out the desirability of the intermediate technology.

The paper also looks at the issue of the choice of products. Concludes that rather than producing a high-quality product such as sugar for consumption by the few, it may be preferable to produce twice the quantity of *gur* (also made from sugar-cane), which is a cheaper, but reputedly more nutritive food. The production of *gur* is also more labour-intensive than the production of white sugar.

54. Duff B, and Estioko I., *Establishing Design Criteria for Improved Rice Milling Technologies.* (International Rice Research Institute, mimeo, 1972).

This paper attempts to assess critically the efficiency and economics of existing rice milling technologies in the Philippines. It also aims at determining the potential for technical improvements in existing systems, and where feasible, the efficacy of initiating activities to design and develop new technologies which will increase efficiency and reduce losses. The existing technologies analyzed are: hand hulling; Engleberg mills; cono-mills; and 'modern' rubber roller mills. Concludes that there is considerable scope for improving the performance of the rice processing industry through modifications to the intermediate-type mills. No major investments in new capital equipment would be necessary.

55. Esmay M.L., 'Drying, Storing and Handling Food Grains in Developing Countries' *Agricultural Mechanization in Developing Countries* (Eds) Esmay M.L. and Hall C.W. (Shin-Norinsha Co.Ltd., Japan, 1973).

Discusses and provides some guidelines for minimizing losses of food grains with proper drying, storing and handling. Looks at drying principles and discusses the advantages and limitations of 7 types of mechanical dryers. Similarly, storage principles and requirements are discussed and examples of several types of traditional and improved storage systems are given.

56. Food and Agriculture Organization, *Improved Storage and its Contribution to World Food Supplies* Development Digest Vol VII (3) July 1969.

Explains how storage facilities can help farmers and gives estimates and causes of losses in stored food in the tropics and sub-tropics. Describes traditional materials used in construction, and gives several examples of the use of new materials.
    See also **Hall D.W.,** *Handling and Storage of Food Grains in Tropical and sub-Tropical Areas.* (FAO, Rome, 1970).

57. Garg M.K., *The Development and Extension of an Appropriate Technology for the Manufacture of Crystal Sugar,* Paper presented at OECD, Development Centre Conference on Low-Cost Technology: An Inquiry into Outstanding Policy Issues. (OECD, Paris, 1975).

Discusses the economic and social impact of modern large-scale technology on the small firms which manufacture traditional sweetening agents like *gur,* and describes the development in India of a small-scale plant for manufacturing the white crystal sugar which consumers increasingly prefer to *gur.* The first pilot plant built in 1957 showed that it was economically and technically possible to manufacture white crystal sugar on a small scale. In the following years, a substantial effort was made to improve this technology. A comparison made in 1973 with the large-scale vacuum pan technology shows that for the same initial investments, small-scale plants using the open pan sulphitation technology can produce 2½ times as much sugar and provide employment for 11 times as many people. The competitiveness of the small-scale technology can be gauged from the fact that plants using this process now account for 8 per cent of India's crystal sugar production and have created some 100,000 new seasonal jobs in the rural areas. These plants, which are set up in the cane-growing areas, allow for substantial savings in transport costs and can be built entirely with local equipment and raw materials.

58. Ghosh B.N., *Drying Cocoa Beans by Gas,* World Crops Vol 25 (5) 1973.

Looks at a new low-cost system for drying cocoa beans, using daily available household gas. The system, which was developed at the Cocoa Research Station of Brazil, is intermediate between sun-drying (which is time-consuming and needs good weather), and sophisticated machines (which are high cost, have excessive breakage rates, have high skill and maintenance requirements, and need very large batches of cocoa beans to be economically viable). Installation costs of the new system are 20 US dollars per square metre of drying floor area.

59. Hewavitharana B., 'Choice of Techniques in Ceylon' *Economic Development in South Asia* (Eds) Robinson E.A.G. and Kidron M. (Macmillan, London, 1970).

Part III comprises a case history of the sugar industry in Sri Lanka (Ceylon). There has been a tendency to imitate the techniques of Queensland and Hawaii where the plants designed are those suited to their conditions of land abundance and labour scarcity. Planning in Sri Lanka has not proceeded in the context of local socio-economic conditions, and the industry has been a failure, with factories operating at only one tenth of capacity. Suggests that a larger number of small plants, each serving 100 to 300 acres of sugar, would have been better suited to local conditions than a few very large mills each serving several thousands of acres. Evidence is that sugar-cane production in small units linked with small manufacturing plants is more appropriate (in terms of unit cost and employment) in conditions approximating to those found in Sri Lanka.

The article also covers paddy cultivation (see entry 21) and the textile and coir industries (see entry 137).

60. Hill P., *A Plea for the Development of Indigenous Methods of Grain Storage in the West African Savannah,* Paper presented at the International Seminar on Change in Agriculture, University of Reading, Sept. 1974.

Describes the many types of traditional style granaries already existing in rural areas, and argues that research should be directed at examining the best types of granaries made in different areas and advising on how these could be improved.

61. International Labour Office, *Sharing in Development: A Programme of Employment, Equity and Growth in the Philippines.* (ILO, Geneva, 1974). Technical Paper No. 8. Mechanization in Agriculture and Agricultural Processing.

Compares three types of rice-mills in the Philippines: the small Engleberg huller mill; the cono-type or under-run disc sheller system; and the 'modern' integrated plants comprising dryers, bulk storage, milling and packaging units. The estimated investment and operational costs for the different rice milling processes are as follows:

	Engleberg Mill	Cono-type System	Modern Mill
Investment costs (pesos)	29,798	86,428	928,444
Fixed operational costs (pesos)	4,420	19,616	174,122
Variable operational costs (pesos)	5,081	28,554	107,018
Unit cost at capacity (pesos)	0.79	0.83	0.30
(Output)	(50 cavans per day)	(240 cavans per day)	(10 metric tons per hour)

At existing market prices for factors, the modern technology apparently has a substantial advantage over the traditional ones. Such figures undoubtedly have been tempting to those who introduced modern technologies. However, low costs at capacity can be consistent with quite high costs when operation is far below capacity and a high share of costs are fixed. The record clearly indicates that, to date, the sort of engineering data presented in the above table have proved misleading under actual operating conditions. (Large mills in the Philippines have been running at about 30 per cent capacity). Also, cost calculations have been made using market prices. The use of shadow prices would favour the traditional (labour-intensive) technologies.

62. **Kilby P.,** *Industrialization in an Open Economy: Nigeria 1945-66,* (Cambridge University Press, 1969).

Chapter 5 looks at four methods being used in 1963 for palm oil extraction. These are: hand method, screw-press, Pioneer Mill, and hydraulic hand-press (in order of sophistication and capital-intensity). Finds that the more labour-intensive methods have generally proved economically more efficient.

63. **Lipton M., Cook I., and Nair N.,** *Cost-Benefit Analysis of Crop Storage Improvements: A South Indian Pilot Study.* (Institute of Development Studies, Discussion Paper No. 56., 1974).

Describes a pilot survey into the size and distribution of cost and benefits of alternative traditional and modern methods of small-scale, on-farm paddy storage in Andhra Pradesh. Most existing loss assessments are 'guesstimates' and rarely related to costings of loss prevention. Hence public investment in small-scale storage improvements, lacking economic 'briefing', has been too low. So has private investment, because private cost benefit ratios understate social ratios, over-reflect risk, and fail to allow for possible scale economies. Improvement requires research into the community aspects of storage decisions, and into the incidence of gains and losses from change.

Five traditional and two improved systems of rice storage were costed and losses in each were estimated. Low rates of return on 'switches' towards somewhat costlier traditional systems, or towards 'modern' 6'' to 9'' concrete bases for some stores, suggest a need for extension and sale of appropriate small-farm devices.

64. **Lockwood L.M.,** *Small Scale Storage and Drying of Paddy in Bangladesh: The scope for reducing losses.* (Working Paper, Appropriate Technology Cell, Agricultural Research Council, Dacca, 1975).

Looks at some current storage and drying practices in Bangladesh and suggests possible improvements. Covers ways of treating grain for small-scale storage, and examines some methods of small-scale drying. Gives estimates of costs and benefits of the proposed changes.

65. **Manalo A.S.** *A Low-Cost Grain Drier,* Paper presented at the Annual Conference of the Philippine Society of Agricultural Engineers, Manila, 1973.

Describes the development of a one-ton capacity low-cost batch drier tailored for local production, and utilizing kerosene or rice hulls for fuel. It was found that the hull extracted from a given weight of paddy could dry 10 times more than its parent paddy weight. The drier costs half the price of a comparable imported batch drier.

66. **National Academy of Sciences,** *Ferrocement: Applications in Developing Countries* (N.A.S., Washington, 1973).

Appendix B looks at the development of cheap, airtight bins made of ferrocement in Thailand. These can hold 4 to 10 tons of grain, other food stuffs, fertilizer, salt, etc., or 2,000 to 5,000 gallons of drinking water. Estimated cost in 1969 was 21 US dollars.

Appendix C looks at ferrocement-lined underground grain silos in Ethiopia. Few traditional pits are sufficiently airtight to eliminate insects, and mould damage is often considerable. Once lined with ferro-cement, however, storage losses in these pits are considerably reduced. Can be made easily with local materials and by local unskilled labour. The cost of a one-ton ferrocement-lined pit in 1972 was estimated at 14 US dollars.

67. **O'Kelly E.,** *Aid and Self-Help.* (Charles Knight & Co. Ltd., London, 1973). Chapter XVI The Corn Mill Societies.

Describes the introduction of small corn mills in the Cameroons in the 1950's. The mills were imported from England and were of a design dating back to the mid 19th century. They were easy to operate, virtually unbreakable, and required very little maintenance. Although they cost only £20, this sum was beyond the means of individual women, so societies were formed. Loans were made available to each society for the purchase of a mill, and the money paid by each member for the use of the mill was used to repay the loan. As the societies became established, and the women had more leisure, they began to ask for classes in such subjects as soapmaking and cookery. The women, with the help of their husbands, built community halls in which these classes were held. Over time, the range of subjects was extended to include child welfare and hygiene, and there was a marked improvement in health in the villages where these societies were located.

68. Pandey M.L. et al., *Efficiency of Different Storage Containers on Seed Quality of Soybeans* Journal of Agricultural Engineering Vol IX (2) June 1972.

Describes results of experiments in India comparing gunny bags, earthen pots, mud bins, bamboo bins with polythene lining, tin containers and steel drums, for soybean storage. Found that the 'intermediate' technology of bamboo bins with polythene lining gave the best results.

69. Parpia H.A.B., 'Transfer and Adaptation of Western Methods in Agricultural Processing' *Alternatives in Development.* (Ed) West J., (SID, European Regional Conference, Oxford, 1973).

Examines how correct selection and adaptation of 'Western' technologies in the field of crop processing can be achieved, and gives examples of the benefits that can result.

70. Patel A.V. and Adesuy S.A., *Crib Storage of Maize under Tropical Village Conditions in the Ibadan Area of Nigeria* Tropical Stored Products Information No. 29, 1975.

Compares the storage of maize in an improved crib (modified to allow better ventilation), and in a silo made of mud bricks with the use of a dryer to reduce moisture to 13 per cent. In the well-ventilated crib, moisture content of the maize decreased steadily from 24 per cent to 13 per cent over a period of 5 months, and if the grain was treated properly, insect damage was as low as 7 per cent at the end of 4 months storage. This was as efficient as storage in a silo, and as the following table shows, the cost of storage in a crib was much less than in a silo.

	Gross grain from storage	Cost of storage	Net grain from storage	Rate of return on investment (six months)
		(Naira)		
Improved crib	114.08	52.00	62.08	113.91%
Village dryer + silo	114.08	84.85	29.23	34.45%

71. **Pingale S.V.,** *Drying Foodstuffs,* Journal of Agricultural Engineering Vol IX (1) March 1972.

Discusses moisture requirements for safe storage of food grains, and describes some current methods of drying them. Details are given of a hot air blower developed in India. This has been extensively tried for drying paddy and has proved to be profitable.

72. **Pradhan S. et al.,** *Pusa Bin for Grain Storage,* Indian Farming November 1965.

Describes experiments at Pusa (Bihar) which showed that storage effects could be much improved if a thin sheet of polythene film was embedded in the mud wall of an ordinary earthen structure. Results were as good as when grain was stored in a much more expensive metallic bin of galvanized tin sheet.
See also entry 79. Wimberley J.E.

73. **Stewart F.J.,** 'Employment and the Choice of Technique: Two Case Studies in Kenya' *Essays on Employment in Kenya* (Ed) Ghai D.P. and Godfrey M. (East African Literature Bureau, 1974).

One of the two case studies is about maize-grinding. Four techniques are compared: hand mills, water-mills; hammer-mills; and imported roller-mills. Variations in product characteristics were found to be the key determinant in the choice of technique. The small-scale 'intermediate' technique — the hammer-mill — was associated with greater employment, output and investable surplus than the more capital-intensive roller-mills. However, the latter were increasingly popular because the product, though more expensive and nutritionally inferior, was widely preferred. Also, the level of capacity utilization was of key importance in determining the relative costs of different techniques.
The other case study refers to the manufacture of concrete blocks. See entry 105, Stewart F.J.

74. **Sutton D.H.,** *The N.I.A.E. Mini-Thresher for Rice, Cereals and Beans.* (National Institute of Agricultural Engineering, Technical Bulletin No. 3. Jan. 1969).

Traditional methods of threshing by beating the grain out or treading with the feet or with animals, give rise to grain loss and damage. On the other hand, mechanical threshers tend to be expensive and difficult to operate and maintain.
This paper describes the development of a machine which would be intermediate between these existing technologies. Characteristics are (1) low price; (2) grain damage not exceeding one per cent; (3) simple design for easy construction in developing countries; (4) lightweight construction for ease of transport. The machine also displaces less labour than more sophisticated threshing machines, needing 5 operators to obtain maximum output of 1,500 lbs of rice per hour.

75.   Tainsh J.A.R. *Farmers Need Mini-Mills,* World Crops Vol 27 (3) July 1975.

The 500 tons of sugar-cane a day mill-tandem was commonplace in the 1930's. However, the benefits of scale effects are such that the economic size has now reached over 6,000 tons for a mill-tandem, while one integrated group of four tandems in Mexico is crushing 20,000 tons per day. For huge milling, transport costs are a problem. Also, there are no large compact areas of good soil left in the world on which can be grown, without irrigation, the million tons or so of cane that the optimum size of modern mill requires each season. There are, however, numerous compact areas of 25 to 100 hectares of fairly fertile land in wet tropical valleys on which rain-fed sugar cane can be grown, or where irrigation is a simple matter of low-lift pumping. The drawback to small-scale production is that existing small-scale mills suffer from the economic handicap of extracting very little sugar from the cane (losses of 40% to 60% are experienced as compared with only 6% in large tandems). This paper describes how the efficiency of mini-mills can be improved, and losses reduced to 15 per cent.

76.   Tainsh J.A.R. *Farmers Need Mini-Mills 2: For the Rice Grower,* World Crops Vol 27 (5) September 1975.

Traditional small paddy mills (e.g. the kiskesan mill in Asia) are highly destructive, with all the rice bran, and much of the rice being lost. The mill with the highest yield of rice and lowest rate of grain breakage is the rubber-roll huller, but this requires large investments of capital. Need to design a huller of low-capital and operating cost, with a rice yield comparable to the rubber-roll.

Describes co-operative 'mini-mills' in Indonesia. These mills accept wet grain paddy from farmers and thus relieve them of the heavy work involved in threshing and drying paddy. Yields are increased because of controlled drying and more efficient milling equipment.

77.   Timmer P.C. *Choice of Technique in Rice Milling on Java,* Bulletin of Indonesian Economic Studies Vol IX (2) July 1973.

Compares five different processing techniques: hand pounding (HP); small rice mills (SRM); large rice mills (LRM); small bulk facilities (SBF); and large bulk facilities (LBF). Finds that, at 1973 wage rates, SRMs are the least-cost facilities for producing value-added in rice processing. The evidence from the countryside, which showed literally thousands of SRMs installed on Java between 1970 and 1973, is thus strongly corroborated by the economic analysis. Only at the extremes of economic conditions (i.e. very low or very high wage rates) could HP or LRMs be explained. The SRMs were shown to be socially and privately optimal over a wide range of circumstances in between.

78.   United Nations Industrial Development Organization, *Essential Oils: A Study of Production Economics* (UNIDO, Vienna, 1973).

Describes and analyses relatively low cost, labour intensive, and simplified technologies appropriate for small-scale essential oil distillation. Describes the machinery and equipment needed for producing oils for different output levels (remaining in the small-scale stage) and compares these units with conventional ones. Covers grass oils, leaf oils, wood oils, flower-petal oils, seed and spice oils, herbal oils, citrus oils, etc.

79. Wimberley J.E. *Storage Practices* Paper presented at the Meeting of Experts on the Mechanization of Rice Production and Processing, Surinam, 1971. (FAO, Rome, 1971).

Describes recent improvements in farm and village storage in India, including the Hapur and Ludhiana metal bins, and the Pusa combination bin with plastic lining. (See also entry 72. Pradhan S.) For larger stores, improvements include raised floors and adequate walls to exclude rain. Urges the use of fumigants. Gives some cost estimates.

80. Wimberley J.E., *Review of Storage and Processing of Rice in Asia.* (International Rice Research Institute, mimeo, 1972).

Throughout Asia, the traditional methods of paddy processing are being replaced with modern techniques and equipment. This paper presents some of the changes and results. It covers harvesting, threshing, drying and storage, parboiling and milling of paddy. Some of the problems of the traditional systems are discussed along with the results of the modern systems.

E. Livestock, Animal-feed, Fishing, Fish-farming and Fishing Equipment

81. Austin V., *Appropriate Technology: Agricultural Engineering,* Paper presented at the University of Edinburgh Appropriate Technology Conference, Sept. 1973.

Includes a case study made in Panama of the rural animal feedstuffs industry, which essentially combines 2 technologies: (1) milling; and (2) mixing grain.

After investigation it was accepted that for milling there were no intermediate technologies between the traditional wooden mortar and pestle, and the modern hammer mill. The choice then became focussed on the range of alternatives analyzed in detail. The capital investment requirements for these were 3,700 US dollars and 2,800 dollars respectively. Up to a discount rate of 10%, the semi-automatic mill was found to be marginally cheaper, and would be selected by a commercial enterprise as the least-cost system. The position would be reversed at higher discount rates. Also, if shadow prices were used instead of market prices, operating costs (particularly for labour) would be significantly lower, and would make the manual system the least-cost choice at all discount rates.

Investigation into the mixing operation revealed that there were intermediate technologies between hand mixing with a shovel, and the simplest of the modern vertical auger-mixers. One simple solution was to take a large drum and insert an axle of 40mm through it diagonally from end to end, and to cut a door of about 300mm by 300mm in the side to allow filling and emptying. The axle could be supported on a simple frame, and driven by hand or animal-power.

82. Dickinson H. and Winnington T.L., *Ferro-Cement for Boat Building* Paper presented at the University of Edinburgh Appropriate Technology Conference September 1973.

Discusses the advantages of using ferro-cement in boat-building and gives details of ferro-cement boat-building in the People's Republic of China. In China, recent improvements in building techniques resulted in a reduction of the selling price of a five-tonne sampan from 800 yuan (£160) in 1966, to 600 yuan (£120) in 1972. Wooden vessels of equivalent type sell at about twice the latter price.

Discusses some experiments with ferro-cement boats in other Asian countries. Technical appendix and useful bibliography.

83. Fish Farming International (Arthur J. Heighway Publications, London.)

Quarterly journal. Includes many articles on fish farming in developing countries. Mainly descriptive and/or technical, but nevertheless gives a useful outline of the state of fish-farming in developing countries, and the problems and advantages involved. Covers equipment for fish farmers.

84. Gale V.E., *World Prospects for Honey Production,* World Animal Review No. 7. 1973. (FAO).

Argues that apiculture has now reached a stage when it should be of considerable interest as an aspect of agricultural development. Its beneficial effects on agricultural ecology, the high labour-intensity needed for processing bee products, the economic use of land and other physical resources, and, lately in particular, the rising world market price for honey, should appeal to administrators and investors alike in many developing countries. Discusses the choice between the establishment of single large-scale apiaries with 1,000 or more hives, and smaller colonies kept by a large number of rural families who could benefit from the additional cash income. Discusses the need for training.

85. Imrie F., *Single-Cell Protein Agricultural Wastes,* New Scientist, May 22, 1975.

Looks at technologies for the production of single-cell protein for feeding livestock. Existing technologies are unsuitable for developing countries because of the high investment cost (£20 to £30 million for an economically-sized plant), the high skill requirements, the high quality of the feed produced (which would have to be exported since no local market exists), and the reliance on the highly technological oil-refining industry. By contrast, a village-level technology has been developed by Tate and Lyle, which involves simple equipment with low capital requirements and uses a minimum of resources. The process recycles agricultural wastes and upgrades them to the level of high-protein chicken and pig feeds to substitute for imported materials.

Includes a case study from Belize in South America. This area was importing pig and poultry feed at a cost of £144 per ton, while the citrus industry was producing 2,300 tons of waste per annum which was simply dumped and was polluting the environment. By using the citrus waste as a substrate for fermentation in a village-level plant, animal-feed (valued at £80 to £100 per ton) was produced. Besides saving foreign exchange, the new technology generated new industry, new jobs, and additional wealth. Only intermediate skills are required in the production process.

86. **National Academy of Sciences,** *Ferrocement: Applications in Developing Countries* (N.A.S., Washington, 1973).

Appendix A describes ferrocement boat-building in a Chinese commune. Workers cited ten superiorities of ferrocement boats over traditional wooden sampans. These included longer life and cheaper maintenance.

In the main text of the book (pp. 4-5), it is stated that 'ferrocement's unique characteristics — low cost of materials, strength, ease of maintenance and repair — recommend themselves particularly to the fabrication of small native craft'.

87. **Palmer-Jones R. and Halliday D.,** *The Small-Scale Manufacture of Compound Animal-Feed.* (T.P.I. Report No. G.67, 1971)..

An economic analysis of 4 different-sized plants for producing animal feed gave the following results:

	A	B	C	D
Scale (output/tons per annum)	2,400	6,000	10,500	16,800
Capital requirements (£)	42,096	105,213	168,236	254,518
Cost per ton (£)	37.3	36.0	37.2	36.5

Finds no significant trend towards lower unit costs as scale increases.
Has a separate chapter on the economics of small-scale production.

88. **Smith D.V.,** *Opportunity for Village Development: The Tanks of Bangladesh,* The Bangladesh Economic Review Vol I (3) July 1973.

Looks at developing fish-farming in village tanks as one possible capital-formation scheme that does not hasten urbanization or village degeneration. Compares two schedules for the use of water in a village tank.

(1) Fullest use is made of the water for irrigation purposes. In this case, the fish must be harvested during the irrigation period from November to January, since there is no water left in the tank after January. This also means that household uses of the tank, e.g. washing and bathing, are terminated until the rains begin to fill the tank in April. Plant growth in the tank is stunted so that fewer decomposed plants are available for next year's fish, and permanent trees around the tank may suffer from a water deficit.

(2) Less water is made available for irrigation, but a minimum depth of water of 2 feet is maintained in the tank for drinking, bathing, and plant growth. This also allows fish harvesting to be spread out over a longer period of time to minimize netting and marketing costs, to allow advantage to be taken of fluctuations in the market price of fish, and to permit scientific harvesting of populations at optimal times, according to fish size.

Recommends fish-farming as a labour intensive and highly productive activity with a schedule that can be adjusted to peaks in labour availability.

89. United Nations Industrial Development Organization, *Boats from Ferro-cement.* Utilization of Shipbuilding and Repair Facilities Series, No. 1. (U.N., New York, 1972).

Points out that there is an urgent need in most developing countries for fishing boats that will help in solving their acute food problems, and for boats that will facilitate transportation in areas where rivers and channels are the most commonly used communication route. Claims that ferro-cement boat-building is perfect for developing countries since it requires a minimum of qualified personnel, imported raw materials and capital equipment. It represents an important alternative to orthodox wooden hulls and to steel hulls. Construction of wood hulls is not always feasible since they require an abundance of well-qualified labour, suitable types of wood which are becoming scarce, and protection from woodworms and other parasites. Steel hulls are not always advisable for small craft, and in any case, they require expensive metal-working machinery as well as highly skilled labour.

Compares the various materials in terms of price, performance, maintenance costs, and life-span. Concludes that ferro-cement compares favourably with the other materials in all respects.

Chapter Five gives advantages and disadvantages of various methods of construction of ferro-cement boats, including a comparison of making an individual hull versus the mass-production of hulls.

Low Cost Housing and Building Materials

90. Boon G.K., *Choice of Industrial Technology: The Case of Woodworking* Industrialization and Productivity No.3. 1961 (U.N., New York)

Includes a comparison of alternative methods of making wooden frames in developing and developed countries. Finds that the choice of technique would be affected by prices of capital and labour, and by the scale of production. In the developed (labour-expensive) country, two special-purpose machines, one performing 4-sided planing and moulding, and the other a double-ended tenorer, were the cheapest combination for output capacities in excess of 50,000 units per annum. In the developing country, however, they would be uneconomic unless capacity exceeded 450,000 unit per annum. Up to an output of 64,000 units, which encompassed the great majority of carpentry workshops, the lowest unit costs would be achieved by using single-ended tenorers and single-purpose planing and thicknessing machines, with considerably lower investment per worker.

91. Bottger J. and Bahr L., *Problems of Uncontrolled Urbanization in the Third World.* (Institut für Tropenbau, Starnberg, 1972). IFT Report No.1.

Questions conventional concepts on the control of urbanization in the countries of the Third World. Particular stress is placed on population mobilization by self-help measures.

92. Demeter H., and Langan T., *Micro-Climate and Comfort in Tropical Buildings.* (Institut für Tropenbau, Starnberg, 1973). IFT Report No.2.

Investigates the effectiveness of tropical construction concepts by analyzing standards of particular buildings in South Vietnam, Tanzania and Mauretania. Concludes that, by a careful consideration of the elements that make up the micro-climatic balance, the enervating consequences of a region's climatic pattern can be alleviated.

93. Fathy H., *Architecture for the Poor: An Experiment in Rural Egypt.* (University of Chicago Press, 1973).

Describes an original approach to rural mass housing in developing countries. The basic philosophy is that 'with appropriate and attractive architectural design, and with someone to show the people in each country how to use their native materials, even the poorest people could have housing that they could construct themselves, that they could afford, and that would serve their indigenous needs while being at the same time socially and aesthetically satisfying'. The author uses a case study from Egypt to prove this point.

94. **Government of India, Ministry of Industrial Development, (Appropriate Technology Cell)**, *Appropriate Technology for Balanced Regional Development* Vol II. Group Studies. (Ed) Behari B. (New Delhi, 1974)

Report of the sub-group on the scaling down of cement plants: covers the techniques of cement production, giving details of 4 existing small-scale pilot plants. Gives comparative cost estimates of these. Finds that unit costs fall as size of plant increases. This is especially true for fuel and labour costs. Concludes that a 2 tonne per day plant would not be economical, but the (still small) 30 tonne and 100 tonne per day plants would be. Recommends where small-scale cement plants might best be located.

Report of the working group on building construction: describes research and work done by various Indian institutes. Covers improvements in brick manufacture, improved lime kilns, and improvements in building productivity.

95. **German Foundation for Developing Countries**, *Development and Dissemination of Appropriate Technologies in Rural Areas* (Ed) Kraetsch R. Proceedings of an International Workshop (GFDC, Kumasi, Ghana, 1972).

Includes two papers on building materials/low cost housing:

Paillon R., *Development of the Tek Block Press:* Describes how the first introduction of stabilized soil blocks to Ghana was unsuccessful, with the expensive Landsborough landcrete machines (U.S. dollars 1,000) tending to remain unrepaired after minor failures. It was decided to reintroduce stabilized soil through a machine similar to the Latin American Cinva Ram, which is simpler in design and operation than the landcrete machine, and costs only 100 U.S. dollars. The modifications which were made to the original machine before its introduction into Ghana are described. Gives the capital and labour costs per block. Concludes that the press is not economical for the building of a single house, but would become economic for 3 houses, and extremely profitable at the scale of 6 houses. This implies the need for co-operation between individual house builders to purchase a machine, or its use by building contractors, or the establishment of a block-making industry.

Beck J., *Low-cost housing for Ghana. Design, Materials, Construction Techniques:* Describes research work done by Kumasi University on improving existing techniques and materials available for rural housing. Includes methods of overcoming water penetration in earth-walled buildings, characteristics of various types of roofing materials, improved designs for doors and windows, reduced-cost sanitary fittings, etc.

96. **Levy C.R.** *The Introduction of Wood Preservation into Papua New Guinea and its Effects on the Rural Community.* (I.U.F.R.O., Abidjan, Feb. 1975).

As villagers gain the means to earn cash incomes, either through cash-cropping or selling their labour, there is an increasing tendency to use more durable building materials. These unfortunately consist of very high cost imported building materials, which while bringing more durable buildings, seldom result in an overall improvement in living conditions. The coolness of grass thatch is replaced with the heat of corrugated iron which, during the often heavy rains, causes such noise that conversation is impossible, and the money spent on these imported goods is lost to the villagers and to the country as a whole. Most villagers seem prepared to put up with the expense and discomforts of new building materials to obtain a durable home, and to free themselves from the never-ending problem of rebuilding their traditional homes.

This paper outlines steps taken in Papua New Guinea to assist the villager to retain the comforts and conveniences of his traditional home, given increased durability of his traditional building materials through the application of techniques of wood preservation. Looks at the dip diffusion process, and at vacuum pressure treatment with copper chrome arsenic (C.C.A.).

97. **Marsden K.** *Progressive Technologies for Developing Countries,* International Labour Review Vol 101 (4) May 1970.

Includes two case studies relating to building materials:

(1)   A case study of inappropriate technological choice in the floor and wall-tiles industry. A ceramic factory making floor and wall-tiles formerly imported hand-operated presses. In cooperation with small engineering workshops in its locality it was able to have replacement presses made locally, using castings, moulded from scrap metal in small foundries and machined on general purpose lathes and drilling machines. The tiles themselves were made of indigenous clay deposits, and fired in kilns composed of local refractory bricks. Thus output, income and employment were stimulated in a number of other industries and trades. This multiplier effect was just beginning to make itself felt when it was decided to build a modern large-scale ceramic plant in place of the existing one, with high-speed fully automatic presses, continuous tunnel kilns, etc. This equipment required special steels and engineering skills, refractories with a high aluminiumium oxide content and technical know-how which were not available locally and had to be imported. Also, because of the high speed of operation, very malleable clays were required, and these too had to be imported. In the end, the consumer got a poorer quality, dearer product because breakage rates were higher due to inadequate temperature control in the tunnel kilns and clumsy handling during the glazing operation. Employment and net output declined in the ceramic and allied industries, and the country's trading deficit widened.

(2)   A case study of a fibreboard plant in an African country showing that an advanced capital-intensive technology is sometimes the most appropriate. The plant cost 2 million dollars and employed only 120 workers directly. However, it processed the residue of sugar-cane and maize stalks which would otherwise have gone to waste. Thus the value added during the process was high and it provided additional income for the farmers. The finished product was a good, cheap substitute for certain kinds of wood for housing and furniture. The wood had previously been imported, so foreign currency was also saved. This project therefore served the national interest in several respects.

The article also includes case studies on leather, footwear, and bread. See entries 125 and 140. Marsden K.

98.   Oliver P. (Ed)., *Shelter in Africa.* (Barrie and Jenkins, London, 1971).

A collection of 16 articles describing traditional forms of shelter throughout Africa using local materials. Suggests ways of improving traditional materials and techniques, and ways of coping with urban populations.

99.   National Academy of Sciences, *Roofing in Developing Countries: Research for New Technologies* (N.A.S., Washington, 1974).

Explores the feasibility of developing new low-cost products and processes with potential for providing roofing materials that offer better performance than those most commonly used today in developing countries. Covers plastics, foam composites, agricultural and wood wastes, ferrocement, etc. Discusses the advantages and disadvantages of each in terms of availability of inputs, skill requirements, durability, costs, etc. Useful addition to existing literature on current roofing materials such as thatch, aluminium and clay.

The use of ferrocement in roofing is also discussed in National Academy of Sciences, *Ferrocement: Applications in Developing Countries,* 1973.

100.   Parikh K. et al., *Performance Approach to Cost Reduction in Building Construction.* (Government of Kerala State, Government Press, Trivandrum, 1974).

Evaluates the cost-effectiveness of different foundation, walling, roofing and ancillary building components and methods in terms of the local situation in Kerala. Among other conclusions, the authors stress that in areas of low labour costs mechanization does not necessarily yield cost advantages. For instance, 'country bricks', produced with handmoulding methods, while four times more labour-intensive, cost less than half as much to produce as bricks from mechanized factories in the same area. The report also gives a qualified endorsement of the small-scale production of lime for use in pozzolanic mortars, while stressing the real opportunity for improving the performance of this and other locally produced materials by sensible quality control methods.

101.   Parry J.P.M., *Review of Prospects for the Manufacture of Permanent Building Materials in the Juba area of South Sudan.* (Intermediate Technology Services/ Regional Development Corporation of South Sudan, July 1975, mimeo).

A report on the potential for the local manufacture of basic building materials in in an area experiencing shortages and high prices of basic walling and roofing materials. Objectives of the project were to (1) examine the requirements for locally produced substitutes for cement-based building materials; (2) examine existing local technology and capacity for bricks and tile manufacture; (3) implement experiments to improve the manufacturing processes with particular regard to improvements in quality and fuel and labour efficiency, and to assess the resultant products; and (4) produce a layout and designs for small-scale brick and tile manufacture, maximizing the use of indigenous materials and skills.

The most important development reported relates to brick-making. The burned clay bricks in current use were found to be irregular in shape, which meant that a lot of mortar was needed to fill the joints. If portland cement was used, this made building very expensive. Alternatively, if mud mortar was used, this softer substance was quickly washed out by rain. It was decided that the problem could be best overcome by the production of even bricks, which would result in smaller joints. The traditional 'slop moulding' process was replaced by a new mould-box, made to the consultants' design, to carry out sand moulding with local clays. Local brick-makers were found to produce good quality bricks with this method after an hour's training.

Also mentions a pilot project for producing soil-cement blocks with Cinva Ram machines; the addition of sawdust and agricultural wastes to tile kilns so as to assist with burning and save firewood; and the introduction of simple wheelbarrows for moving bricks between the drying area and the kiln.

102. Pawley M. *Garbage Housing, U.S.A.* Architectural Design Vol XLV (3) 1975.

Looks at 2 basic constructional methods using beer and soft drink cans, giving illustrations of full-sized residences built in New Mexico. The building of these houses led to the development of a new cottage industry in the area, whereby local people collected cans and wired them up in their homes, using a home-made jig, to produce the required 'building blocks'.

103. Sadove R., *The Minimum Standard Approach to Housing and Related Services* Development Digest Vol XII (3) July 1974.

Argues for replacing high cost home construction programs with lower cost sites and services projects in which occupants build their own homes. Cites Calcutta as an example of a city where 87 per cent of households could not afford repayments on a loan for a 'low-cost' or 'minimum' dwelling. Includes a case study of a settlement scheme in Senegal as a successful example of a site and services project.

104. Small Industry Development Network, *Mini Cement Plants: An Alternative Approach.* SIDN Newsletter, Vol 1 (4) 1975.

The trend, even in developing countries, has been towards larger cement plants, in which any saving are offset by higher transport costs. This article asks is there an alternative to large-scale production of portland cement. Concentrates on modern vertical kilns, which have been modified to overcome some of the disadvantages inherent in earlier versions. Such disadvantages included variations in quality and an inability to operate continuously.

The advantages of modern vertical kilns over rotary kilns are: (1) they occupy only one seventh of the space; (2) they can operate on solid fuels and a variety of wastes; (3) they can be located in areas where transport bottlenecks prevent the setting up of large plants; (4) they can be located near potential markets to save transport and packing costs; and (5) investment costs per ton are only half as great.

Describes the installation of a 2 ton-per-day capacity vertical kiln and a 30 ton-per-day capacity kiln in Jorhat, India. Concludes that efforts to establish large modern cement plants should be coupled with a movement toward the installation of several mini-cement plants so as to effect greatest economy and do more in less time with less capital.

105. Stewart F.J., 'Employment and Choice of Technique: Two Case Studies in Kenya' *Essays on Employment in Kenya* (Eds) Ghai D.P. and Godfrey M. (East African Literature Bureau, 1974).

One of the 2 case studies is on concrete block making. Five techniques are compared: hand-operated block-makers; small stationary vibrating machines; large stationary vibrating machines; small laying machines; and large laying machines. All but the first two types of machine are imported. Variations in product characteristics were found to rule out the hand block-making technique for multistorey buildings. Choice of technique was also influenced by the scale of output, with the more labour-intensive techniques being more efficient at low scales of output, but not at high.

See also Stewart F.J. 'Manufacturing of Cement Blocks in Kenya', *Technology and Employment in Industry.* (Ed) Bhalla A.S. (ILO, Geneva, 1975).

106. Strassman W.P., *Mass-Production of Dwellings in Colombia: A Case Study.* (Working Paper, International Labour Office, Geneva, 1974).

Looks at the choice between high-rise and low-rise buildings. Finds that ultramodern methods are the most viable for high-rise apartments, but that cheaper, more labour-intensive methods can be used for low-rise buildings. The lower cost of site per dwelling for high-rise buildings was not sufficient to compensate for the much lower construction costs of low-rise apartments:

	1 Storey	4/5 Storeys	30 Storeys
Cost of site per dwelling	US$1,643	US$ 707	US$ 227
Cost of construction per dwelling	US$3,857	US$5,572	US$7,714
Total cost per dwelling	US$5,500	US$6,279	US$7,940

Also makes a case for self-help technology, because of a lack of sufficient resources to build complete houses for more than a small proportion of poor people.

107. Turner J.C., *Barriers and Channels for Housing Development in Modernizing Countries,* Journal of the American Institute of Planners Vol XXXIII (3) May 1967.

Uses a case study of a squatter settlement on the outskirts of Lima to prove the hypothesis that the standards required by the authorites conflict with the demands of the mass of urban settlers. Official housing projects attempt to telescope the development process by requiring minimum modern standard structures and installations prior to settlement. Such 'instant development' procedures aggravate the housing problem by disregarding the economic and social needs of the mass of urban settlers in modernizing countries. On the other hand, the procedures followed by self-selecting occupant builder communities, free to act in accordance with their own needs, enables the synchronization of investment in buildings and community facilities with the rhythm of social and economic change.

108. Turner J.C. and Fichter R. (Eds). *Freedom to Build* (Macmillan, New York, 1972).

A collection of 9 articles, including many case histories, which show that where dwellers are in control, their homes are better and cheaper than those built through Government programs or by large corporations. Of particular interest are:

Grenell P., *Planning for Invisible People: Some Consequences of Bureaucratic Values and Practices:* looks at urban policy in Indian cities, and compares bustee improvement schemes with the development of new towns.

Terner I.D., *Technology and Autonomy:* an extremely thorough article covering all aspects of technology for housing, including intermediate technologies such as small, simple and standardized brick, block and mat components.

109. United Nations, Department of Economic and Social Affairs, *Use of Bamboo and Reeds in Building Construction.* (U.N., New York, 1972).

Bamboos and reeds are the oldest and chief building materials in rural areas and villages throughout the world's tropical and sub-tropical regions. They are popular because they are plentiful and cheap, can be used by villagers to build their own homes with simple tools, and there is a living tradition of skills and methods required for construction. Houses constructed from these materials are easily built, easily repaired, well ventilated, and earthquake resistant. However, a major drawback to their use is deterioration by insects, rot, fungi and fire. Untreated bamboo structures usually have to be replaced every two or three years, and this means that there is little incentive to install interior toilets, indoor water supplies, interior cooking facilities, etc. Improvements in material properties and construction techniques would thus enable millions of rural dwellers to have an improved standard of living. The report covers preservative treatments such as coating (with tar, limewash, etc.), dipping (in oil, etc.), and steeping pressure treatment.

110. United Nations, Department of Economic and Social Affairs, *Self-Help Practices in Housing: Selected Case Studies.* (U.N., New York, 1973).

Reviews 5 case studies from Colombia, El Salvador, Senegal, Ethiopia and the Sudan, describing experiences in the field of self-help and mutual-aid housing. Concludes that no other form of housing programme could bring adequate housing to such a large proportion of the population, and that self-help housing methods have a considerable potential for mobilizing human resources for the provision of homes for low-income families.

111. United Nations Industrial Development Organization, *The Establishment of the Brick and Tile Industry in Developing Countries.* (U.N., New York, 1969).

Surveys the range of technologies available at each stage of brick-making, and comments on the appropriateness of each for developing countries.

112. **United Nations Industrial Development Organization,** *Production Techniques for the Use of Wood in Developing Countries.* ID/WG. 49/10. (UNIDO, Vienna, 1969).

Discusses technical and economic aspects of building with wood under conditions existing in developing countries. Covers improvements in material properties and construction techniques.

113. **United Nations Industrial Development Organization,** *Construction Industry,* (UNIDO, Vienna, 1969). UNIDO Monograph on Industrial Development, No.2.

Based on studies and papers presented to the International Symposium on Industrial Development convened by UNIDO in Athens 1967. A broad study covering only the salient features of the industry, with particular reference to the problems of developing countries.

114. **United Nations Industrial Development Organization,** *Building Materials Industry,* (UNIDO, Vienna, 1969). UNIDO Monograph on Industrial Development, No. 4.

Based on studies and papers presented to the International Symposium on Industrial Development in Athens in 1967. Reviews the trade and production of the industry, assesses trends in consumption and patterns of use. Further chapters outline the characteristics of the industry and give guidelines on planning and organization.

Section 3

Manufacturing

A. Food Processing and Nutrition

115. Armas Jr. A., *Implications of Legislated Minimum Wages on the Choice of Technique in the Agro-Canned Pineapple Industry in the Philippines: A micro-approach,* Papers and Proceedings of the Workshop on Manpower and Human Resources (University of the Philippines, School of Economics and National Economic and Development Authority, Laguna, 1972).

An example of 'adaptive' technology transfer. Finds that due to lower wages, the pineapple canning industry in the Philippines uses three times as much labour as its 'original' counterpart in Hawaii. Canning is done by hand in the Philippines and the product is of a higher quality than in Hawaii.

116. Campbell M., *Stable Tropical Fish Products.* (International Development Research Council, Ottawa, 1975. IDRC 041e.)

Deals with improvements of traditional salted/dried fish products in tropical countries of South East Asia, and with the development of non-traditional products using minced fish obtained from trawler by-catches. Such by-catches, which are currently vastly under-utilized, are estimated to be 400,000 tons per annum and 200,000 tons per annum in Thailand and India respectively.

117. Cooper C. et al. 'Choice of Techniques for Can Making in Kenya, Tanzania and Thailand', *Technology and Employment in Industry.* (Ed) Bhalla A.S. (ILO, Geneva, 1975).

Looks at 17 alternative techniques for manufacturing cans. In the three countries studied, capital-intensive techniques were used not merely because other more appropriate techniques were not available; more appropriate techniques did already exist, but they were simply not used in situations in which it appeared that their use would have been justified. Gives several examples of inappropriate choice of technique. Concludes that policies designed to adjust distorted factor prices would have been ineffective in changing the choice made since in some cases the relatively labour-intensive (intermediate) techniques were already the most economical at existing wage rates. Suggests that steps should be taken to reduce or eliminate various randomly distributed forms of imprudent selection of techniques, and to reduce the influence of the factors that insulate decision-making from local prices and costs.

50

118. Hall M.N.A., *The Small-Scale Manufacture of High and Low Boiled Sweets and Toffees.* (Tropical Products Institute Report No. G.77., 1973).

Compares three scales of output in West Africa. Results are summarized in the table:

	A	B	C
Output (tons per week)	less than 1.0	5.00	20.00
Capital (£)	9,000	54,000	165,000
Unit cost (£ per lb)	0.099	0.081	0.076
Direct labour per ton	5.00	3.00	2.75

Finds that unit costs decrease as scale of output increases, but points out that all three plants are 'small' in that they do not require heavy investment in high-speed fully automatic machinery and large market outlets.

Chapter 4 on 'Choice of Scale' discusses the use of second-hand machinery.

119. International Labour Office, *Employment, Incomes and Equality: A strategy for increasing productive employment in Kenya.* (ILO, Geneva, 1972). Technical Paper No. 7. 'A Case Study of Choice of Techniques in Two Processes in the Manufacture of Cans'.

Looks at the choice of techniques for the sealing and packaging of cans using data obtained from a Kenyan factory where each of these processes is carried out by both capital-intensive and labour-intensive methods. Findings were as follows:

	End Sealing		Packaging	
	Automatic	Semi-Automatic	Automatic	Semi-Automatic
	(Kenyan shillings per 10,000 cans)			
Capital costs ($r = 20\%$)	3.71	0.152	1.30	0.35
Labour costs	2.70	9.14	1.30	4.34
Total costs	6.41	9.29	2.60	4.69

Concludes that although semi-automatic techniques are not inefficient in the formal sense (i.e. there is no technical rigidity in the normal sense of the term), their labour and capital productivities are too low compared to those of the automated techniques to make them viable at any realistic shadow wage rate. (In fact, the critical wage rate would be below the opportunity cost of unskilled labour.) They are a vintage of techniques which have been overtaken by capital-intensive technological change. Points out that the main problem in the case of semi-automatic sealing is the high requirement for supervisory labour, which results in high labour costs. Stresses that some labour-intensive processes may demand very little skill and consequently require much less supervisory labour than does the can-sealing process. As a general rule, therefore, the use of such processes cannot be ruled out *a priori*.

120. **Kamath J.,** *Small-Scale Manufacture of Soluble Coffee.* (Tropical Products Institute Report No. G.82., 1973).

Compares the cost of manufacture of soluble coffee at three different scales of production in India. Findings are summarized in the table:

	A	B	C
Output (Kg. per hour)	75.0	225.0	400.0
Cost per Kg. (pence)	2.4	2.3	2.3
Fixed Investment (£)	786,900	1,598,900	2,300,900
Return on Capital (%)	0.2	24.0	29.0

Concludes that only the 2 larger plants are economically viable, and that these cannot be defined as 'small-scale'. For instance, plant B requires £286,000 just for plant and equipment, whereas the Indian definition of small-scale production is under £41,574 for plant equipment. However, the report goes on to show that certain modifications to production, e.g. the mixing of chicory with coffee, and the use of glass containers only, would result in economic viability of the small-scale plant. The former modification would give a return on capital of 13 per cent for plant A, while the latter would give a return of 23 per cent.

121. **Kamath J.,** *Small-Scale Manufacture of Carbonated Beverages.* (Tropical Products Institute Report No. G.65., 1971).

Comparison of 3 different size of plants operating at full capacity in Nigeria gave the following results:

	A	B	C
Output (bottles per annum)	500,000	2,000,000	5,000,000
Capital (N.£)	7,580	23,170	42,180
Return on capital (%)	−7	59	100

Shows that the smallest-scale plant is not economic, but adds that it could break even under conditions of very low wage rates. Also, if output is restricted to 50% capacity, the medium-scale plant would make a loss, while the rate of return to capital for the large-scale plant would be reduced to 10 per cent.

122. **Kaplinsky R.,** *Innovation in Gari Production: The Case for an Intermediate Technology.* (Institute of Development Studies, Discussion Paper No. 34., 1974).

Examines the choice of techniques in the processing of gari from cassava in Nigeria.

Two techniques are contrasted: (1) a fully-mechanized foreign machine; and (2) an intermediate, locally-generated technique. Calculations suggest that unit costs of production are approximately 20 per cent higher with the mechanized than with the intermediate technique. Concludes that both private and social optimality are furthered by the use of the intermediate technique.

123. Kilby P., *African Enterprise: The Nigerian Bread Industry.* (Stanford, 1965).

Gives data on six firms in the bread industry of different sizes, with different market orientations, and using different technologies. Finds that the firm at the lowest technological level economizes on capital but has high total costs because of the high raw-material content; while the technically most advanced firm minimizes losses in the production process but has trouble with spare parts, power failures, high fuel costs, and finding skilled supervisors. There is also a limited market for its product so that it operates below capacity.

124. Mars P.A., *The Manufacture of Orange Squash in Developing Countries.* (Tropical Products Institute Report No. G.53. 1971).

Looks at costs and profits per unit at different levels of output in West Africa, so as to reach a decision as to the most appropriate scale for the existing market. Comparison of 4 different sizes of factories gave the following results:

	A	B	C	D
Output (100 doz. bottles p.a.)	128	256	512	1,020
Sales cost (£ per 100 doz. bottles)	130	111	105	105
Transport costs (£ per 100 doz. bottles)	4.6	2.9	2.0	2.2
Manpower (men per 100 doz. bottles)	22.5	13.3	9.6	8.2

Shows that unit costs fall as the scale of output increases, and that transport costs, being subject to their economies of scale, follow the same trend as total costs. However, the report accepts that a small or moderate sized firm might be viable in some circumstances, e.g. on an island, or in a very remote community. Refers to cottage-scale (less than 10 employees) orange-squash manufacture in Nigeria, and suggests that these small firms survive by employing family members, and charging very low prices to a limited number of customers.

Also covers choice of machinery e.g. between automatic and manually operated juice extractors, giving costs and capacities of each.

125. Marsden K., *Progressive Technologies for Developing Countries,* International Labour Review, Vol 101 (4) May 1970.

Includes a case study on the choice of technology in the bakery industry. An automatic plant bakery, with pneumatic flour handling, continuous mixing, kneading, dividing and proving, a travelling oven and conveyor-fed wrapping machine, costing 4 million dollars and employing 100 men, could supply all the bread for a town of 100,000 people. But if the average income were only 100 dollars per head per annum, and savings were only 10 dollars per head, the whole of the town's savings would go into the new bakery and the mass of workers in other trades and industries would have to make do with less equipment than they had before (because of depreciation). Demand would also fall because of the reduced incomes of the redundant bakery workers. Thus total output and employment in the town would decline.

If on the other hand, the existing small bakers were supplied with simple dough kneaders to replace hand-mixing, at a total capital cost of 10,000 dollars, the average labour productivity in the bakery industry could be raised by 10 per cent and there would be plenty of savings left over in the community to finance further investment in the other sectors where marginal increases in productivity could be achieved too. And there would be improvements in the social amenities of the town, e.g. schools and hospitals, etc. Thus, growth would be balanced and mutually self-supporting.

Article also includes case studies on leather, footwear, ceramic tiles and fibreboard. See entries 97 and 140. Marsden K.

126. McDowell J., *Development of High Protein/High Calorie Biscuits in Uganda Using Indigenous Protein Sources,* East African Journal of Rural Development. Vol 6 (1&2) 1973.

A case study of an attempt to provide a nutritionally-significant contribution of high quality protein and sufficient calories to supplement effectively existing diets of children. The problem is to provide nutrients in a very concentrated form so that only a small bulk need be eaten. Biscuits were decided upon as being suitable, and they had the additional value that they could be given the image of a 'children's food', so that they were less likely to be eaten by male adults. Describes the difficulties which had to be overcome in the baking technology, and looks at problems of packaging and acceptance.

127. Ngoddy P.O., *The Case for Appropriate Technology in the Mechanization of Gari Manufacture in Nigeria,* Paper presented at the OECD, Development Centre Conference on Low-Cost Technology: An Inquiry into Outstanding Policy Issues, (OECD Development Centre, Paris, 1975).

A comprehensive case study of the mechanization of gari (dehydrated cassava) production. Describes the traditional household technology, the intermediate technology, and the large-scale production technology. A detailed economic and technical comparison is made between the large-scale and the intermediate technologies. Both are found to have advantages and drawbacks, and the conclusion reached is that the relative competitiveness of each one depends on the economic assumptions which are made about such factors as interest rates, shadow price of labour, number of hours of operation per day, wage and foreign exchange rates, etc.

128. National Academy of Sciences, *Food Science in Developing Countries: A Selection of Unsolved Problems.* (N.A.S., Washington, 1974).

Aims at identifying ways in which science and technology can be applied appropriately to the areas of nutrition, food processing and the development of new foods. Covers iron fortification of salt, reducing spoilage of food, processing fermented fish products, indigenous sources of enzymes for rapid fermentation of fish, keeping qualities of buffalo milk, salt for preservation purposes, development of techniques for making bread without wheat, and development of local low-cost weaning foods. Useful bibliography and list of contacts on each topic.

129. Selowsky M. and Taylor L., *The Economics of Malnourished Children: An Example of Disinvestment in Human Capital,* Economic Development and Cultural Change. Vol 22 (1) October 1973.

Estimates the economic impact of infant malnutrition in Santiago, Chile, dealing particularly with its implications for adult productivity. Suggests that (1) early malnutrition leads to intelligence loss in children; (2) because of their low intelligence on entering school, the retarded children receive somewhat lower 'quality' education, leave school earlier, etc; and (3) when they enter the labour force, they are doubly handicapped by lower intelligence and less schooling. As a result they earn less money. The measure of benefits resulting from alleviating malnutrition is based on the imputed earnings foregone by the adults who suffered from malnutrition in infancy in comparison to another group of adults who were not malnourished.

130. Spata J.A. et al., *Developing a Soybean Dal for India and Other Countries,* World Crops Vol 26 (2) 1974.

Discusses techniques for processing soybeans into a dry, stable 'dal'. The product has a similar appearance to indigenous dals, and can be stored and cooked in a similar way. The processing equipment is very simple, and the market price of the product appears to be competitive. The resulting food is higher in protein and fat content than normal dals.

131. Spurgeon D., *Anyone for Instant Yams* IDRC Reports Vol 4 (2) June 1975.

Describes the development of a pilot plant in Barbados to produce instant dehydrated yam. The purpose of this is to make good use of native root crops, to help attainment of self-sufficiency in food, and to diversify exports away from the traditional sugar crop. Other developments mentioned include a breakfast food like corn-flakes made from sweet potato flour enriched with soya protein, and the use of composite flour (20% yams or 15% sweet potatoes) in breadmaking.

132. Tropical Products Institute, *The Small-Scale Manufacture of Confectionery.* (T.P.I. Report No. 14/60. 1960).

Looks at the costs and labour requirements of manufacturing high-boiled drops in a factory with a capacity of 10 cwt of fruit-drops per day. Recommends that wrapping of sweets should be done by hand, since machines are expensive and have a high capacity. In 1960, the smallest machine available could cope with half a ton of sweets per day. In addition, if sweets are wrapped by hand, then 12 workers are needed to produce 10 cwt of sweets per day, as opposed to only 2 workers if a machine is used for wrapping.

133. United Nations Industrial Development Organization, *Wood as a Packaging Material in Developing Countries.* (U.N. New York, 1972).

Concentrates on the use of wood for packaging agricultural produce. Chapter Five examines the various technical processes and looks at the choice of machinery for producing nailed cases and pallets, light, oblong packing cases, and wirebound cases. Gives comparative costs and outputs involved in each process, and points out that the choice of technique should depend on the size of output envisaged, the degree of standardization necessary, the amount of investment required, and the cost of labour.

A very wide range of alternative techniques is described for each process. For example, the assembly of cases and pallets ranges from nailing by hand, through portable stapling machines (200 to 1,500 dollars) and stationary nailing machines (1,000 to 2,000 dollars), to an automatic nailing line (100,000 dollars) which should be used only when very large outputs are required.

B. Clothing, leather and footwear

134. Bhalla A.S., *Investment Allocation and Technological Choice: A Case of Cotton Spinning Techniques,* Economic Journal September 1964.

Compares three technologies for the spinning of cotton; the labour-intensive 'traditional' charka; the 'intermediate' Ambar charka; and the capital-intensive factory spindle. The traditional charka has the lowest capital/output ratio and the highest capital/labour ratio, while the factory spindle yields the highest reinvestable surplus. Concludes that either of these is preferable to the 'intermediate' technology.

135. Dickinson H., *Rural China, 1972.* (Report prepared for the Commission on the Churches: Participation in Development, World Council of Churches, Edinburgh, 1972). p.34.

One of the more novel technological innovations described in this interesting report is the feeding of silkworms on cassava leaves to produce a coarse variety of silk.

136. Howes M. and Hislop D., *The Transfer of Technology to the Thai Silk Industry* (Science Policy Research Unit, University of Sussex, mimeo, 1974).

Contains three case studies of technological alternatives:

(1) *Alternative Strategies for the Development of Thai Silk:* describes a number of alternative production strategies; introduces criteria by which these alternatives

may be evaluated; and attempts to explain the rationale which lies behind the decisions that have been taken in Thailand, and which have led to a less than optimal utilization of national manpower and material resources.

(2) *Technology Transfer in the Thai Silk Industry — a Study of Problems and Alternatives:* covers much the same ground as the first study, but with much greater emphasis on economics. Diagram showing the relationship between increasing complexity of machinery (covering 8 types of machine) and thread quality. Finds that the capital cost of machinery in the most complex system is almost 20 times greater than that in the most labour-intensive method. It also involves only 1 worker for every 33 workers needed in the labour-intensive method.

(3) *Success and Failure in the Transfer of Technology — The Case of Thai-Japanese Sericulture Programmes:* examines an attempt to adapt existing technology to the local environment. This is used to illustrate some of the more general problems which can arise, and suggestions are given as to how they might be overcome.

137. Hewavitharana B., 'Choice of Techniques in Ceylon' *Economic Development in South Asia* (Eds) Robinson E.A.G. and Kidron M. (Macmillan, London, 1970).

Part II looks at the characteristics of alternative techniques in textile production. Findings are summarized in the table:

	Hand Loom	Decentralized Power Loom	Automatic Power Loom
Cost per yard (Rs)	1.85	1.60	1.50
Volume of output per worker per year (yds)	1,154	7,232	79,200

Although a move from hand looms to automatic looms would result in some saving in unit cost of production, the number of jobs destroyed could not be justified in social terms.

Reaches the same conclusion for the coir industry. At the decortication, spinning, and mat weaving stages, a move towards more highly mechanized techniques would lower the unit cost of production, but if the most mechanized techniques were used at all stages, in preference to the least mechanized, then even a doubling of output would not reabsorb all the labour displaced.

138. International Labour Office, *The Role of the Textile Industry in the Expansion of Employment in the Developing Countries.* (ILO, Programme of Industrial Activities, Textile Committee, Report II, 1973).

Chapter IV comprises a general discussion of the technology and investment options in the textile industry in developing countries, and looks at their consequences for employment. A case study of the modernization of the textile industry in Indonesia is included in Chapter VI.

139. Lockhart-Smith C.J. and Elliot R.G.H., *Tanning of Hides and Skins.* Tropical Products Institute Report No. G.86. 1974).

The main report compares 4 scales of output of hides. The results are shown in the table:

	A	B	C	D
Output (hides per day)	100	400	1,000	2,000
Total capital investment (£)	61,000	255,000	638,000	1,172,000
Cost per m^3 (£)	2.11	1.96	1.88	1.80
Profit (%)	2.29	12.31	18.14	25.10

This shows considerable economies of scale in production. An appendix on the tanning of goat and sheepskins reaches the same conclusions.

140. Marsden K., *Progressive Technologies for Developing Countries* International Labour Review Vol 101 (4) May 1970.

Includes two case studies of inappropriate technological choice in the leather and footwear industries:

(1)   One country imported two plastic-injection moulding machines costing 100,000 dollars each. Working three shifts and with a total labour force of 40 workers, they produced 1½ million pairs of plastic shoes and sandals a year. At two dollars per pair, these were better value (longer life) than cheap leather footwear at the same price. Thus, 5,000 artisan shoemakers lost their livelihood which in turn reduced the markets for the suppliers and makers of leather, hand tools, wax and polish, laces, etc. As all the machinery and the material (PVC) for the plastic footwear had to be imported, while the leather footwear was based largely on indigenous materials and industries, the net results were a decline in both employment and real income within the country.

(2)   A tanning industry project in one country envisaged building a small model tannery to act as a training centre and to demonstrate new techniques, together with a number of new buildings to rehouse existing tanneries, thus improving working conditions and separating the industry (with its obnoxious smells) from living quarters. Total capital costs were projected at 2½ million dollars for an annual output of 15 million dollars. The buildings and some of the machinery were to be made locally so the import content was small. Labour productivity was expected to increase, but the number of workers employed in the industry would remain at 3,000 owing to a 5 per cent per annum expected increase in demand for leather.
    However, the project was referred on the grounds of not being modern enough, and was replaced by a scheme for a large Govenment-owned tannery-estate, costing 15 million dollars, equipped with the latest imported machinery, and with a total capacity 50 per cent in excess of the existing firms. Employment in the industry would be halved, existing equipment made obsolete, owners of present firms made redundant, and the import bill increased by 8 million dollars.

141. McBain N.S. and Pickett J., *Low-Cost Technology in Ethiopian Footwear Production,* Paper presented at OECD, Development Centre Conference on Low-Cost Technology: An Inquiry into Outstanding Policy Issues. (OECD, Development Centre, Paris, 1975).

Presents the results of an economic appraisal of alternative technologies for the manufacture of footwear in Ethiopia. Three levels of output are considered: 50,000, 300,000, and 1.8 million pairs of men's shoes per year. For each of these three levels of output, the authors have considered three different technologies: the most machine-intensive, the most labour-intensive, and the least-cost. A comparison between these 9 theoretical production units shows that the most machine-intensive process is not the most profitable, even though engineers may prefer it for technical reasons.

The second part of the paper assumes that Ethiopia wants to produce 1.8 million shoes for export. This can be done with one large factory, with 20 medium-scale factories, or with 1,200 small workshops. If economic efficiency is the over-riding criterion, the large-scale factory, based on the least-cost technology, and not the most machine-intensive technology, appears to be the most suitable. Evaluations are on the basis of private profitability, and the authors point out that a social cost-benefit evaluation would probably favour the smaller units and the more labour-intensive techniques.

142. Pack H., 'The Choice of Techniques and Employment in the Textile Industry' *Technology and Employment in Industry* (Ed) Bhalla A.S. (ILO, Geneva. 1975).

Looks at the rationality of considering utilizing older, used equipment when undertaking investment in textile industries in developing countries. Suggests that at factory prices relevant for many poorer countries, the choice of used equipment would be optimal. Existing older-style equipment does offer efficient labour-intensive alternatives, and is available in large quantities in used form. Though it is not possible *a priori* to rule out the potential generation of still more efficient labour-intensive techniques if sufficient research funds were available, it is far from clear that the effort would be warranted by a cost/benefit analysis.

143. Powell J.W., *A Review of Experience gained from 3 Projects at the Technology Consultancy Centre, University of Kumasi, 1972/3,* Paper presented at the University of Edinburgh Appropriate Technology Conference, September 1973.

Includes a description of a project to encourage the use of broadlooms for weaving. The main barrier to using broadlooms was one of cost. They retail at approximately C. 100.000 as opposed to only C. 7.00 for a traditional loom. The Centre decided to test the acceptance of weavers to a loan scheme by which a broadloom was supplied and paid for in 20 monthly instalments of C. 5.00. The first of the broadlooms purchased through this scheme have yielded a good return and loans have been repaid ahead of time. The resulting increase in demand for broadlooms and their associated equipment has led to the establishment of a local enterprise to manufacture these. Training schemes for operators have been run concurrently at the College of Art.

The other projects described are Spider Glue and Steel Bolt Production. See entry 160. Powell J.W.

144. Ranis G., *Technology Choice, Employment and Growth.* (Yale Economic Growth Center, Discussion Paper No. 97. 1970). p.16.

Shows that a capital-intensive technology, while being profitable in Europe or North America, may not be profitable under conditions of much lower wage rates prevailing in other countries. Uses an example from the Japanese textile industry to make this clear. 'The price of the automatic loom in Japan is more than twice as much as the plain loom, which with the additional expense involved in the importation from the U.S.A. or Great Britain, made the total outlay too high in a country where the interest charges on money were relatively much higher than the cost of labour. Japanese mill managers have, therefore, hitherto preferred to employ more workers and to forgo the more labour-saving but more expensive machinery, in contrast to the situation in the U.S.A., where the high-priced labour is economized rather than the machinery.'

145. United Nations Economic Commission for Latin America, *Choice of Technologies in the Latin American Textile Industry.* (UNECLA, 1966).

Compares three vintages of mill — 1950, 1960, and 1965 (each containing a spinning and a weaving section) — with each mill being more capital-intensive than its predecessor. Concludes that given the low availability of capital in Latin American countries, maximum benefits in terms of reinvestable surplus, return on capital, and employment creation are attained by the use of the 1960 (the intermediate) vintage.

146. United Nations Industrial Development Organization, *Report of Expert Group Meeting on the Selection of Textile Machinery in the Cotton Industry* (UNIDO, Vienna, 1967). ID/WG 8/1.

Presents quantitative data for the hypothetical mill process flows for carded cotton. These are conventional, intermediate, and automated. The conventional level was found to be the most appropriate for developing countries, with the automated level being the least appropriate.

147. United Nations Industrial Development Organization, *Wet Blue Chrome Leather for Export* (UNIDO, Vienna, 1971). ID/WG. 79/3.

Contains a discussion of the possibilities of improving the technologies used by cottage and small-scale tanners so as to raise the quality of their products to export standards. Looks at the organizational problems involved.

148. United Nations Industrial Development Organization, *Seminar Report on the Development of the Leather and Leather Products Industries in Developing Countries: Regional Project for Africa* (UNIDO, Vienna, 1972).

Covers modernization and mechanization of small enterprises to produce shoes for international markets.

C. Other Manufactured Goods

149. Boon G.K. 'Technological Choice in Metalworking, with Special Reference to Mexico', *Technology and Employment in Industry,* (Ed) Bhalla A.S. (ILO, Geneva, 1975).

The author uses process of task-level analysis and argues that it is only at this high level of disaggregation that possibilities of factor substitution can be satisfactorily revealed. Moreover, private enterprises make decisions largely at this level of disaggregation. The empirical disaggregated analyses on metalworking confirm the existence of capital-labour substitution possibilities, even though, at a higher level of aggregation, the technologically-determined view of fixed proportions seems to prevail.

150. Cooper C., Kaplinsky R. and Turner R., *Second Hand Equipment in a Developing Country: A study of jute-processing in Kenya.* (ILO, Geneva, 1974).

A case study relating to machines in a jute-processing factory in Kenya. It examines (a) how purchases of second hand machines are made, and particularly how prices are determined; and (b) how the performance of second hand machines compares with the performance of similar machines that were bought new by the same enterprise. This is aimed at giving some useful pointers about the actual advantages and disadvantages of second hand equipment.

There are 3 major conclusions. First, it is difficult to hold a general position about second hand machines. Some are an efficient way of saving capital, and others are not. Second, the price at which the second hand machines are purchased is often a rather poor indication of the capital saving that they make possible. The machines have to be transported and installed, and the costs involved are the same as for new machines. If these costs are too high, the entrepreneur in the developing country should not buy the second hand machines, even if the machine price is low. And third, the real problem for the machine owner is to obtain a reliable estimate of the rate of output of second hand machines. This is difficult because the effect of lifting and transportation on machine performance is unknown, and because there is a wide variation of performance between machines in a second hand vintage. These findings lead the authors to advocate a more discriminating attitude towards the whole question of imports of second hand machinery.

151. Date A., *The Manufacture of Miniature Cigars.* (Tropical Products Institute Report No.G.15. 1965).

Covers hand-making of full-size cigars, hand-making of miniature cigars, and machine manufacture. Production of 20 cigars per hour per individual hand worker could be doubled to 40 cigars per hour per worker using a moulding machine, can be increased by automatic machines to many hundreds per hour/worker, or even to many thousands per hour, according to type and size of unit being produced. Suggests that there might be scope for setting up a small, non-automated cigar factory, aimed at a small local market. This could be profitable in situations of low labour costs.

152. **Edwards D.,** *The Industrial Manufacture of Cassava Products: An economic study.* (Tropical Products Institute Report No. G.88. 1974).

Covers the production of chips and pellets, and production of starch. Compares two sizes of factory producing chips (inputs of one ton of tubers per hour, and 7 tons of tubers per hour); and two sizes of pelleting plant (inputs of 2.5 tons and 5.0 tons of dried chips per hour) in Malaysia. Finds that economies of scale exist for production of both products.

In the case of starch processing, three sizes were considered: throughput of one ton per hour (simple machinery); throughput of 2 tons per hour (continuous processing); and throughput of 6 tons per hour (continuous processing). The continuous processing system was found to have a reasonable rate of return only in the larger-scale plant, and only at full utilization of plant. For output at a small-scale, the enterprise using simple traditional equipment was found to have an economic advantage over the small continuous processing plant.

153. **Foster P. and Wood D.,** *The Case of Small Fertilizer Plants in India,* Development Digest Vol. VI. (2) April 1968.

Compares the costs and returns of one large plant and seven small plants of combined capacity equal to the large plant. Finds that it would take 7 years before the annual net returns from the large plant exceeded those from the small ones. Advantages of small-scale production were: (1) small marketing area; (2) less demands on management; and (3) much shorter construction time with consequent savings in interest charges and imports of fertilizers and grains.

154. Garg M.K., *Problems of Developing Appropriate Technologies in India,* Appropriate Technology Vol. 1. (1) Spring 1974.

Includes a case study of a pilot pottery project in India aimed at assessing the commercial viability of small-scale enterprises. The background to the project was that the supply of 'traditional' domestic and kitchen utensils manufactured by village potters was being replaced by white-ware porcelain articles manufactured through large-scale techniques in the cities. As a result, more than one million potters in India were facing the prospect of being thrown out of employment. The pilot project, aimed at the manufacture of white-ware pottery for villages, has been worked out in two stages. The first is a cluster of small-scale decentralized units which have grown into quite a sizeable complex employing more than 25,000 people in 200 to 250 units, and producing about £5 million worth of goods annually. The other development has resulted in making small units work in isolated villages.

155. Intermediate Technology Services Ltd., *Techno-Economic Feasibility Report on Mini-Plants in Pakistan* (ITDG, London, 1974 mimeo).

A report written for the Government of Pakistan. Contains an evaluation of the feasibility of intermediate processing technologies in rural Pakistan. Covers: (1) the feasibility as a village fuel of methane produced by the anaerobic fermentation of animal and vegetable wastes; (2) local, small-scale sugar processing; (3) the production of protein concentrates from grasses and other leafy greens; and (4) the utilization of various types of agricultural wastes.

156. **International Labour Office,** *The Woodworking Industries and the Creation of Employment* (ILO, Programme of Industrial Activities, Second Tripartite Meeting for the Woodworking Industries, Report II, 1975).

Chapter IV looks at the choice of technique in the woodworking industries in developing countries, and examines the possibility of substituting labour for capital in production. Also, compares the 'modern' sector with the 'traditional' or 'informal' sector, and argues that greater social benefit could be achieved by concentrating investment on the latter sector. Gives several examples of ways in which the quality of output and productivity in the 'traditional' sector could be improved without resort to major investments in capital. Covers 'intermediate' technologies and the use of second-hand machinery.

157. **Kamath J., Flynn G., and Mars P.A.,** *The Manufacture of Woven Sacks from Natural and Synthetic Fibre.* (Tropical Products Institute Report No.G.90. 1975).

Although jute has been the most widely used fibre for the manufacture of sacks, this report concentrates on kenaf, because conditions for growth are more widespread, and it is more likely to be used by developing countries planning to manufacture sacks, rather than import them. Compares 4 plants in Thailand which produce: (1) heavy cees on flat looms; (2) heavy cees on circular looms; (3) hessian sacks on flat looms; and (4) polypropylene sacks on circular looms. All plants work 3 shifts, and produce 10 million sacks per year.

Reaches three major conclusions. First, heavy cees woven on circular looms cost more than those woven on flat looms. This illustrates that it does not usually pay to install labour-saving machinery in developing countries, where labour costs are low. The circular loom costs 10 times more, but has a productivity only 3.7 times greater, and provides 141 less jobs. Second, the manufacture of heavy sacks on plain looms has a considerable advantage over the manufacture of heavy cees, but it is doubtful if they could compete wih polypropylene. These sacks cost only half of the hessian sacks, and one third of the heavy cees. And third, polypropylene sacks should be made on flat looms, which is technically feasible. This would reduce quality slightly, but there would be a saving in capital costs, and more jobs would be created.

158. **King K.,** *New Light in Africa: Kenya's Candlemakers,* Paper presented at the University of Edinburgh Appropriate Technology Conference, September 1973.

A case study of the developments in a low cost industry — the manufacture of the small paraffin wick lamp that sells in Kenya for 50 to 70 cents (2½ new pence). The cheapest alternative is the hurricane lamp, imported from Hong Kong, China and Czechoslovakia, which costs at least 14 times as much, and burns paraffin at 3 to 4 times the speed of the small indigenous lamp. The lamp is made principally out of reworked and soldered motor oil cans, with a removable wickholder and a separate small funnel for refilling with paraffin. It gives enough light for most household purposes, and is remarkably accident-proof.

159. Powell J.W., *Soap Pilot Plant — Review of the First Year's Progress* (Technology Consultancy Centre, University of Science and Technology, Kumasi, Ghana, 1973); and *Soap Pilot Plant Project — Review of Progress in 1974* (TCC, Kumasi, 1975).

These two reports describe the setting up and progress of a soap pilot plant following from a stream of enquiries from small soap makers as to how the unpleasant odour and colour which remained in their soap from the vegetable oil could be removed. The plant, which was conceived as an exercise in intermediate technology, was intended to improve qualitatively and quantitatively upon the operation of the small local soap makers, but without making the plant too complex for them to understand and control. The plant is planned to produce 1,000 bars of soap per day — a daily production of 2,500 lbs of soap. The product has been well accepted by local traders, and so far production has proved profitable. However, profitability is dominated by the cost of palm oil, and if the price of this continues to rise, profits could fall.

In the soap making process, caustic soda in 10% aqueous solution is an important input. Due to the alarming shortages of this input at the time of starting the soap plant, it was decided to construct a small plant for the manufacture of caustic soda. Development and operation of this prototype has been troublefree, and some firms ordering small soap plants from the Centre have also ordered a caustic soda plant. Details of the caustic soda plant can be found in Donkor P. and Serviant G., *Report on the Local Manufacture of Caustic Soda* (Technology Consultancy Centre, UST, Kumasi, 1974).

For other work done at Kumasi, see entry 160. Powell J.W.

160. Powell J.W., *A Review of Experience Gained from Three Projects at the Technology Consultancy Centre, University of Science and Technology, Kumasi, 1972/3,* Paper presented at the University of Edinburgh Appropriate Technology Conference, September, 1973.

Describes three projects started by the Centre in 1972 with the aim of applying the technological expertise of the University in the development of local industries.

(1) *Spider Glue:* A small manufacturer of cassava starch requested to be taught how to make a good quality paper glue. To make glue from starch is fairly simple (an alkali obtained from plantain peel is mixed with cassava starch), but to obtain a good quality glue, suitable for re-wetting and capable of being stored, requires the addition of chemicals and some technical expertise. The technical problems were solved and·the final product is judged to be equal in quality to imported glues. The business is now flourishing, initial bank loans (which were secured with help from the Centre) have been paid back, and the Centre's fee for advice has been paid back in full. Also, the foreman of the original enterprise has now left to set up his own business.

(2) *Steel Bolt Production:* Since steel bolts made by local blacksmiths were of a poor quality, and imported bolts were too expensive, wooden lorry body builders expressed a need for good quality bolts to be manufactured locally. Some bolts were produced, but it was found that the lorry body builders were unwilling to pay more than the 10 pesawas per bolt that was charged for the blacksmiths bolts, even though imported bolts were costing 25 to 30 pesewas. The project would have folded at this stage but for enquiries for hexagon headed engineering bolts. These were then produced and found to cost only half as much as imported bolts and were superior in strength. In July 1972, a Steel Bolt Production Unit was established as an independent unit within the Faculty of Engineering, and in 1973, the Unit was transferred off campus to a private entrepreneur.

(3) *Broadloom Weaving:* See entry 143. Powell J.W.

161. Reynolds G.F., *The Ox-Plough Revolution,* Chemistry in Britain Vol 8 (12) December, 1972.

Discusses intermediate chemical technology. Points out that what can be done depends on local conditions and on available materials, but, in general, the objective should be first to produce basic materials or chemical compounds, and then to use these in simple manufacturing processes. Choice should be governed by the following criteria: (1) processes should be simple and involve the minimum of equipment; (2) power requirements should be small; (3) processes should be labour-intensive and (4) they should be batch processes and capable of operation on scales from very small to medium size.

Small power supplies discussed include wood, charcoal and methane (produced from biological materials). An interesting application of methane in 'intermediate technology' is its use as a fuel for the Humphrey pump (water pump introduced into England at the beginning of the century). Simple chemical processes discussed include caustic soda and the manufacture of soap; processes based on wood; products from seaweed; and products from sugar cane.

See also Reynolds G.F., *Appropriate Chemical Technology for Developing Countries* Paper presented at the University of Edinburgh Appropriate Technology Conference, September, 1973.

162. Robbins, S.R.J., *The Manufacture of Dry-Cell Batteries.* Tropical Products Institute Report No. G.46. 1970).

A high proportion of the operations involved in dry-cell battery manufacture may be performed either on hand-lines, or using semi-automatic machinery. The report looks at this choice of technology for 3 basic 1.5 volt cells: R20, R14, and R6 (penlight cell). Gives costs and yields for 12 plants based on factor costs prevailing in a West African country in 1969. Concludes that there should be a core of semi-automatic machinery for producing the most popular cell (R20), and that hand-lines can be utilized for the less popular types. At the time, the smallest available semi-automatic line had a capacity of 5 million units per annum, while hand-lines could economically operate at a capacity of a quarter of a million units per year.

163. Schwartz S.L., *Second-hand machinery in development: or how to recognize a bargain,* Journal of Development Studies Vol 9 (4) 1973.

Examines the theoretical implications of the availability of both new and used machines for the production possibilities and effects of various trade policies on the selection of production technique. Integrates the question of new versus used machines with investment criteria, and examines situations in which used machinery might be preferable to new.

164. Tabour H., *A Solar Cooker for Developing Countries,* Solar Energy Vol X (4) Oct/Dec. 1966.

Describes a durable solar cooker designed specifically with a view to fabrication in centralized workshops in developing countries. Except for the 12 identical 29.3 cm. diameter concave glass mirrors, the construction is entirely of iron, and the total cost is under 8 U.S. dollars. Long-life (the mirrors last for 4 years and the cooker for 10 years), simplicity for user, and negligible maintenance are important features, Although the cooker is not the cheapest that can be designed, the very high durability is expected to more than compensate for the additional initial cost. The cooker can boil 1¾ litres of water in 22 minutes.

165. United Nations Economic Commission for Asia and the Far East, *Small Industry Bulletin for Asia and the Far East.* (U.N. New York, annual).

Recent articles of interest include:

1971: Food Processing Industries in India.

1972: Manufacture of Electric Motors; Manufacture of Dry Cell Batteries.

1973: Leather Tanning and Leather Goods Manufacturing — An important small-scale industry in India; Chemical and Allied Industries in India — Scope and Direction; Rural Industrialization and Rural Electrification — the Indian Experience; Small modern industry in Malaysia.

1975: Technology in Small Business — Problems and Solutions

166. Wells Jr. L.T., *Men and Machines in Indonesia's Light Manufacturing Industries,* Bulletin of Indonesian Economic Studies Vol IX (3) Nov. 1973.

Gives the results of the author's survey of a number of manufacturing plants in Indonesia in 1972. This was aimed at determining the reasons for the choice of technology which was in use. As the table shows, a considerable range of technology was encountered in all six industries:

Number of Plants by Technology and Industry

	Plastic Sandals	Cigar- ettes	Soft drink Bottling	Bicycle Tyres	Flashlight Batteries	Woven Bags	Total
Capital- intensive	2	3	1	1	2	2	11
Intermediate	6	5	3	4	2	2	22
Labour- intensive	0	3	2	1	4	0	10
Total	8	11	6	6	8	4	43

In general, intermediate technology provided 3 times as many jobs for the same output as the capital-intensive technology; and the labour-intensive technology provided 10 times as many jobs as the capital-intensive technology in the same industry.

The author found there was no simple relationship within an industry between factor costs and the technology chosen. Nor did the choice of technology appear in all cases to represent a simple attempt to minimize costs. Further, no significant relationship was found to exist between the choice of technology and whether the firm was foreign or domestically owned, quality of output, or scale of operations. Choice was found to be most closely related to the competitive position of the firm. If a brand image allowed the firm to hold a monopolistic position, then managers were influenced by non-economic factors, such as the ease of management with capital-intensive methods, and the preference of engineers for sophisticated equipment. When price was an important consideration, however, then there was a tendency to use more labour-intensive methods, which were profitable due to low wage rates.

See also Wells Jr. L.T. *Economic Man and Engineering Man: Choice of Technology in a Low Wage Country,* Paper presented at the Ford Foundation Seminar on Technology and Employment, New Delhi, 1973. .

Section 4

Infrastructure

A. Power Sources

167. Bailey P.H. and Williamson W.F., *Some Experiments in Drying Grain by Solar Radiation* (National Institute of Agricultural Engineering, U.K., undated).

The direct use of solar energy to replace conventional heat sources is intrinsically desirable to conserve the world's limited resources of fossil fuel. Equipment to make use of solar energy for some purposes tends to be elaborate and expensive, and in industrial countries, it is usually more economic to use conventional fuels. In underdeveloped areas, however, transport costs often make the price of coal and oil prohibitive for many purposes, and direct use of solar energy holds a particular attraction. The use of a solar air heater for supplying warm air to a relatively sophisticated drier for grain offers a marked advance on primitive open-air drying, but a certain amount of mechanical complication is implicit in such equipment. This paper gives attention to methods of drying grain in which the radiation is collected directly by the material to be dried, thus reducing costs and complexity.

168. Directorate of Gobar Gas Scheme, *Gobar Gas: Why and How?* (Khadi and Village Industries Commission, Bombay, undated).

Works out the costs and returns on construction of a 60 cubic feet gas plant. Finds that it is more profitable to pass cattle dung through a gobar gas plant than to convert it directly to either dung cakes (for fuel) or farm yard manure. Also has incidental advantages of hygienic operations, absence of smoke and soot, convenience in burning, and richness of manure.

169. Dryburgh P. McA., *Charcoal and Other Products from the Thermal Decomposition of Wood.* (University of Edinburgh, mimeo, 1974).

Attempts to suggest some lines of action which might be taken on the development of charcoal-making at some different technological levels, with particular reference to the possibility of obtaining useful by-products by simple means. The three scales considered are (1) one-man pit operation; (2) a more developed operation run by a small community; and (3) a major chemical plant processing many tons of wood per day and obtaining a range of by-products.

Concludes that simple kilns offer a real improvement for one-man charcoal operations, but that by-product recovery at this level is not worthwhile. At the intermediate scale, however, the preparation of activated charcoal and the recovery of wood-tar could be valuable processes, and the use of wood-tar in road making and wood preservation are worth investigation. Finally, the economic and ecological implications of a major wood-distillation industry should be examined for the case of a particular country, with a view to designing a suitable plant.

170. Garg M.K. *Short Studies on the Development of Appropriate Technology for Home Living in Rural Communities,* Paper presented at OECD, Development Centre, Conference on Low-Cost Technology: An Inquiry into Outstanding Policy Issues. (OECD, Development Centre, Paris, 1975).

Includes a review of the development of bio-gas plants in the last 40 years, both in India and in other selected countries. Cattle dung currently accounts for over 25 per cent ot India's energy consumption. The fermentation of dung in a bio-gas plant produces methane, which is used for cooking, lighting, etc., and the residue is used as manure. The diffusion of this well tested technology has not been widespread owing to the high cost relative to other sources of energy. However. recent rises in the price of imported oil have given a big boost to the diffusion of cowdung cookers.

171. Golding E.W., *Windmills for Water Lifting and the Generation of Electricity on the Farm* (Agricultural Engineering Branch, Land and Water Development Division, F.A.O. Informal Working Bulletin, No. 17).

Concentrates on wind power for agricultural use on farms which have little immediate prospect of connection to main power networks, or where difficulty in transporting fuel may render mass-produced power expensive. Concludes that the use of windpower, if it is to be economical, is not merely a question of buying a machine and installing it anywhere, for subsequent operation. Many factors such as climatic, topographical, economical and social, should be taken into account if a wind power project of significant size is to be carried out successfully. Deals separately with wind power for direct water pumping, and the generation of electricity by wind power. Looks at small units for single isolated premises, and at medium-sized plants for isolated communities.

172. Johnston P., *Appropriate Technologies for Small Developing Countries* (Smoothie Publications, Brighton, 1974).

The first part of this monograph concentrates on renewable energy sources. Includes a survey of the costs and benefits of 3 types of windmill, and compares windpower with diesel engines in various uses. Also looks at developments which could reduce the costs of using solar energy to a point where it becomes feasible for small-scale needs.

The second part of the paper gives examples of (1) the scaling down of petroleum refineries, and of plants for making steel and producing ammonia; and (2) the development of technologies at the 'intermediate' level — particularly in the chemical industry.

Has an extensive and useful bibliography.

173. Kuppuswamy M., *Cereal Drying with Solar Heat,* Paper for the Proceedings of a Seminar on Post-Harvesting Technology for Cereals and Pulses, (Indian National Science Academy, New Delhi, 1972).

Discusses the possibility of utilizing solar heat for producing hot air needed in a mechanical drier. Describes a workable go-down roof which is designed to serve both as a solar heat collector and as the roof covering material. Looks at how to work out the most economical roof area.

174. Little E.C.S., *A Kiln for Charcoal Making in the Field,* Tropical Science Vol 14. 1972.

Describes a new type of metal, transportable charcoal kiln known as the CUSAB. This enables light, useless scrub to the rapidly converted into charcoal, which can be sold, e.g. for domestic fuel. By this technique, necessary bush clearing can proceed at a profit (a trial in Kenya cleared whistling thorn trees at a profit of 50 pence per acre for the whole operation); and large trees, conventionally used for charcoal production, can be spared.

175. Makhijani A.. *Energy and Agriculture in the Third World.* (Ford Foundation, Energy Policy Project Report, 1974).

Argues that the Third World needs a mixture of 'big' technology and 'alternative' technology. A comparison of some decentralized systems with current methods of providing energy for agriculture, primarily in the form of oil and electricity, reveals that in many instances the decentralized approaches are less costly, while in others the centralized approach is more appropriate. Makes recommendations about various energy technologies that should be pursued for the developing nations. 'An urgent program of research and development of solar energy technologies must be launched by Third World countries, with the co-operation of the oil-exporting nations and the industrialized countries if possible'. Pyrolysis of wood 'may be an economic approach to providing fuel for small towns'. Bio-gasification, which is 'perhaps the most important technology for converting biological material to more useful forms of fuel' should be vigorously pursued.

176. Merriam M., *Windmills for Less Developed Countries,* Technos Vol 1. (2). April 1972.

Sets out the conditions which should be considered in order to decide whether a windmill would be the most economical source of energy for a particular locality. This includes consideration of availability and cost of animal draught power, and the cost of diesel power, in relation to that of wind power.

177. Moorcraft C., *Solar Energy: Plant Power,* Architectural Design Vol XLIV (i) 1974.

Examines the potential use of plants for solar energy conversion, and argues that research in this area would be of far greater immediate practical benefit to society than other current growth areas of solar energy research (e.g. the photo-thermal and photo-voltaic conversion of solar energy into electrical energy). Also covers sewage farming and the use of kitchen wastage for production of methane.

178. National Academy of Sciences, *Solar Energy in Developing Countries: Perspectives and Prospects.* (N.A.S. Washington, 1972).

Gives 4 important reasons for considering solar energy resources to meet the needs of developing countries: (1) most developing countries are in or adjacent to the tropics and have good solar radiation available; (2) they do not have widely distributed, readily available supplies of conventional energy resources; (3) energy is a critical requirement in developing countries because it is related to the production of housing, clothing, food and agricultural and industrial production; and (4) most developing countries are characterized by arid climates, dispersed and inaccessible populations, readily available labour, and a lack of investment capital.

Covers solar evaporation, water heating, distillation, refrigeration, conversion to mechanical or electrical energy, cooking, etc. Describes experiments and developments in these fields in various parts of the world.

179. Parker R. N., 'The Introduction of a Powersaw into the Charcoal Burning Industry: A Study in a Savanna Village in S.E. Ghana'. *Agriculture in S.E. Ghana. Vol. II.* (Eds) Dalton G.E. and Parker R.N. (University of Reading, Department of Agricultural Economics and Management, Development Study No. 13. 1973).

A description of the charcoal burning industry and its importance in the economy of a village in the South Savanna area of the Volta Region, Ghana, preceeds an investigation of a possible method of increasing productivity. The only innovation showing promise was the introduction of a powersaw which it was hoped would simultaneously eliminate the arduous task of felling trees, and raise returns of labour of the charcoal burners. Reaches the conclusion that: (1) the powersaw led to a 10.4 per cent reduction in felling charges; (2) the powersaw made felling services more available; (3) the powersaw operation is one of the few enterprises that a person with some initiative can enter to build up wealth rapidly. A direct benefit/cost ratio of 1.64 was calculated as a result of the introduction of a powersaw.

180. Parkes M.E., *The Use of Windmills in Tanzania.* (Bureau of Resource Assessment and Land Use Planning, University of Dar-es-Salaam, Research Paper No. 33. 1974).

Both general use and particular use of windmills in Tanzania are discussed. Various types of windmill are mentioned and their expected performances presented. From an analysis of relevant wind data, the potential for windmill use is assessed and predictions given for expected performances in 2 general locations. Recommendations for windmill use in rural water supply, cattle watering, and irrigation are derived. Annual costs for the largest size of windmill and for the equivalent diesel-powered unit are compared. Designs for windmills which could be made locally are discussed, as well as the possibility of local manufacture of conventional windmills.

181. Prasad C.R., Prasad K.K., and Reddy A.K.N., *Bio-gas Plants: Prospects, Problems and Tasks,* Economic and Political Weekly, Vol IX Nos 32-34, Special Number, August 1974.

A detailed case study of whether bio-gas plants will fulfill the demand for decentralized energy and fertilizer production, particularly in a large number of small Indian villages which, on economic grounds, are going to be by-passed in the rural electrification programmes. Shows that in a village of 500 persons, 250 cattle, and 100 houses, despite a 75 per cent dung collection efficiency, a low bio-gas yield of 3 cubic feet per lb. dry dung will provide a total energy of about 667.5k.W.h. per day at a generating cost of about 5 paise per k.W.h. This energy output is over 30 per cent more than the 500 k.W.h. per day now consumed by such villages from both commercial and non-commercial energy sources. Further, the bio-gas energy output is sufficient for 10 pump-sets, 5 industries, one light in every home, energy for cooking in every house, and a variety of miscellaneous purposes. In contrast, rural electrification programmes are only targetting for about 100 k.W.h. per day, thus compelling the continued use of non-commercial fuels, and as a consequence, the continued loss of fertilizer and forest through the burning of dung and firwood. A cost/benefit comparison of bio-gas energy versus rural electrification comes out in favour of the former.

Further, the bio-gas plants produce about 295 tonnes per year of organic manure, corresponding to about 4.4 tonnes of nitrogen per year from which the minimum additional yield of food grains may be expected to be about 22 tonnes. This fertilizer output is more than the village's requirements on the basis of current average consumption of nitrogen per hectare. Also, fertilizer production from bio-gas plants appears to have several advantages over production from large-scale coal-based plants from the point of view of the saving of capital and the generation of employment.

182. Richard C., *Recycling or Pollution,* South Pacific Bulletin Vol 24 (3) 1974.

Describes a scheme for converting animal excreta into useful by-products such as methane gas and green algae. Estimates that enough gas can be produced per day per pig to cook enough food for one person. The green algae, which grow on the surface of the oxidization pond can be harvested, and being rich in protein, make valuable food for livestock. After oxidization, the water is excellent for breeding ducks and fish, and the outflow of water from the ponds can be used to irrigate vegetable gardens or corn fields. Initial expenditure on the system is less than 1,000 Australian dollars and can be recovered in one or two years.

183. Sigurdson J., *The Suitability of Technology in Contemporary China,* Impact of Science on Society Vol XXIII (4) Oct/Dec. 1973.

Looks at small-scale power generation in China. Covers exploitation of small, scattered coal deposits; small and very small hydroelectric power stations (35,000 stations ranging from a few kilowatts to a few hundred kilowatts provide 16 per cent of China's hydroelectric power); the proliferation of small rural enterprises able to manufacture simple generators and electric turbines (some equipment is made of bamboo and wood instead of iron so as to keep costs in moderation); modifications in electricity distribution (e.g. wide spacing of poles) to lower costs; and, in areas remote from electricity, the popularization of simple methods to produce marsh gas (methane) for cooking and lighting (e.g. by fermentation of grass and straw in sealed pits).

Also looks at small heavy industry in local areas e.g. nitrogen chemical fertilizer, cement (using vertical kilns), and pig iron production.

184. **Smith G.**, *Economics of Solar Collectors, Heat Pumps and Wind Generators.* (University of Cambridge, Department of Architecture, Autonomous Housing Study, Working Paper No. 3., 1973).

An economic analysis of the power systems currently available for utilization in an autonomous house. Uses investment analysis and discusses the appropriate rate of interest. Tries to divide current costs into components so that high cost problem areas can be enlightened. Concludes that solar collector costs are high, but lower costs may be achieved by using passive collection and storage systems, or by annual storage, which may become economic in the future with rising fuel costs.

185. **Steedman N.**, *Eire's Emerald Energy*, Architectural Design Vol XLV (6) 1975.

Looks at the growing of an 'energy crop' on the bogs of Ireland for burning to generate electricity. Some 130,000 acres are currently used for the harvesting of peat and the 11 turf-burning power stations produce 24 per cent of the country's total electricity. However, the same quantity of electricity (1,750 million units) could be generated per annum if the same area were used to grow an energy crop (which unlike peat would be renewable) at 1 per cent photoynthesis efficiency for burning at 30 per cent thermodynamic efficiency. At these efficiencies, it is calculated that 765 square miles (2.8 per cent of the land area) could provide all of the country's electrical energy requirements, and that 3,125 square miles (11.3 per cent of the land area) could provide all of the country's primary energy requirements.

Also has a brief section on experiments with wind power in Eire.

186. **Stessels L. and Fridmann M.** *Use of Solar Energy for the Conservation of Coffee in Humid Regions,* Café, Cacoa, Thé. Vol 16 (2) 1972.

Describes work in Madagascar to develop a simple device designed to maintain, at low cost, optimum hygrometric conditions in green-coffee warehouses. Gives results of tests with experimental installation in 1970, including costs of storage.

187. **Tabour H.**, *Solar Energy for Developing Regions.* (UNESCO, Working Party on Solar Energy, Paris, June 1973). Sc-73 Conf. 801/2.

It is possible to perform successfully a wide range of tasks using solar energy, but these processes are not normally viable on economic grounds. Solar energy is free, but its collection and conversion is expensive and capital intensive. This paper discusses developments in the areas of solar water heaters, solar distillation, solar cookers, driers and refrigerators, etc., and describes recent developments and attempts to overcome complexities and high costs. Concludes that a shortage of capital and psychological factors (preventing acceptance), rather than technology, are the major stumbling blocks to more widespread use of solar energy in developing countries. In cases where the capital outlay is not excessive or where alternatives are either non-existent or difficult in a particular locality, solar devices are already being used.

188. United Nations, *New Sources of Energy: Proceedings of the Rome Conference, 1961.* Vols 4, 5 and 6, Solar energy; Vol 7, Wind power. (U.N. New York, 1963).

Gives numerous examples of the use of solar energy and wind power for various purposes in several developing countries.

189. United Nations Department of Economic and Social Affairs, *Small Scale Power Generation: A Study for Pioneer Electrification Work; An Overall Review of Methods and Costs of Power Generation, with Particular Emphasis on Small-Scale Generating Plants for Pioneer Electrification Work in Developing Countries.* (U.N., New York, 1967). ST/ECA/94.

Looks at costs of various types of power generation including generating plants run on gas, steam, water and wind. Part Four looks at the special problems relating to small power plants, while Part Five gives several case studies of small plants in developing countries. Concludes that although electricity generated by means of small power plants may sometimes be very costly, by comparison with electricity sold in large modern cities, this does not necessarily mean that it should be ruled out as uneconomic. Although cheapness is desirable and conducive to rapid growth, it is not the only consideration, and it will often be preferable to have costly electricity than no electricity at all.

190. United Nations Department of Economic and Social Affairs, *Solar Distillation as a Means of Meeting Water Demands.* (U.N., New York, 1970). E. 70. II. B.1.

Aims at defining the conditions under which solar distillation may provide an economic solution to the problem of fresh water storage in small communities. Reviews current status of solar distillation, and provides a method for potential users to estimate performance and costs of current still designs in their areas.

B. Water Supplies and Sanitation

191. Aris D., *Low-cost Rural Water Systems in Guatemala,* Development Digest Vol 5 (3) October 1967.

A case study of how new technologies have made it possible to provide water to all buildings in a rural area at low cost. The technologies involved are a cut-off device that can be fitted into water faucets, thus limiting water use by individual households; and the use of newly developed plastic pipe which is expected to result in a saving of 60 per cent in cost over imported galvanized steel pipe.

192. Bureau of Resource Assessment and Land Use Planning, *Rural Water Supply in East Africa.* (Ed) Warner D. (BRALUP Research Paper 11. University of Dar-es-Salaam, 1969).

A fairly general collection of papers, the majority of which cover the health and technical aspects of water supplies. Appropriate technologies include:

Barker P.W., *Butyl Rubber Sheeting in Water Conservation and Storage.*

Cotter G., *The Shinyanga Lift Pump:* describes a simple inexpensive hand pump constructed from locally purchased materials and designed to tap the high ground water table in the Western Shinyanga region of Tanzania. The total cost to a village for a 5 feet deep well, well-cover and pump in 1969 was 130 shillings.

193. Bureau of Resource Assessment and Land Use Planning, *Water Supply: Proceedings of the Conference on Rural Water Supply in East Africa.* (Ed) Tschannerl G. (BRALUP Research Paper 20. University of Dar-es-Salaam, April 1971.

Deals with some of the key issues in water development in East Africa. Papers include:

Bateman G.H., *Intermediate Technology and Rural Water Supplies:* Argues against large irrigation schemes and in favour of developing simple technologies for water supplies in rain-fed areas. Includes a case study of the mud/polythene, sausage method of constructing rainwater catchment tanks. Concludes that although the cost per unit volume of water is greater for catchment tanks than with other sources e.g. dams and boreholes, the catchment tanks have the advantage of providing water at just the place it is needed, and their construction lends itself to self-help.

Irvin G., *Problems of Benefit/Cost Analysis in Planning Rural Water Supply:* Looks at the difficulties involved in measuring the benefits resulting from investment in rural water supplies.

Matango R.R. and Maylerle D., *The Experience with Rural Self-Help Water Schemes in Lushoto District:* Examines the costs and benefits of 19 self-help water schemes.

194. Carruthers I.D., *The Contribution of Rural Water Investment to Development,* East African Journal of Rural Development Vol 3 (2) 1970.

A case study which looks at the potential health and economic benefits accruing from rural water improvement. The method used is to compare one area with piped chlorinated water with another area, similar in all respects, except for the provision of piped water. Concludes that if maximum economic gains are sought then investments should be concentrated in areas that have a high degree of development. This is so that any additional labour which becomes available through improved health can be profitably employed. Also finds that although individual water connections may be thought desirable, this may not be sufficient to ensure that potential health and economic benefits will be realized. There will also be a need for general hygiene and environmental improvements and better medical facilities.

195. Carruthers I.D., *Impact and Economics of Community Water Supply: A Study of Rural Water Investments in Kenya* (Wye College, Agrarian Development Unit, 1973).

Although most developing countries are committed to large rural water investment programmes, there is a dearth of literature on the impact and economics of such investment. This study aims at integrating the various technical, engineering, agricultural and medical aspects of investment in potable water systems, using an economist's approach. Points out that the complexities preclude the use of formal cost/benefit analysis, but other concepts and techniques are relevant and necessary if resources are to be judiciously allocated. Discusses the choice between individual connections and communal points, and cites several empirical studies of impact of water schemes, including some examples of self-help schemes. Major conclusions are that:

(1)   either low-cost, low-impact communal point systems should be installed initially, or high cost, high benefit individual connection systems, rather than the present high-cost communal networks.

(2)   potential health and economic impact of investment in potable water supply is substantial, but realized benefits are insignificant. This is because of a neglect of complementary facilities such as health and agricultural education, agricultural credit, and production and marketing programmes. Argues that in many instances the potential opportunities can be exploited at very low cost, often at only the cost of conveying information.

196. Frankel R.J., *Appropriate Technology for South-East Asia: Series Filtration Using Local Filter Media,* Paper presented at the OECD, Development Centre Conference on Low-Cost Technology: An Inquiry into Outstanding Policy Issues. OECD, Development Centre, Paris, 1975).

Describes the development of a suitable technology for water filtration and purification, based on the local resources of South-East Asian countries. Gives the results of tests on various simple filter media such as shredded coconut husks, burned rice husks, gravel, and charcoal. The author concludes that such filtering technologies are both inexpensive and appropriate, representing a feasible alternative to the complex and high-cost technologies of the industrialized countries.

197. Garg M.K., *Short Studies on the Development of Appropriate Technology for Home Living in Rural Communities,* Paper presented at OECD, Development Centre Conference on Low-Cost Technology: An Inquiry into Outstanding Policy Issues. (OECD, Development Centre, Paris, 1975).

Contains two case studies of appropriate technology for rural water supply and sanitation. The argument underlying both is that villagers and farmers should have at their disposal the same sort of amenities as the urban population:

(1)   Village water supply system: The technology originally developed consisted of purifying the village water well by automatic chlorination — a pot full of bleaching powder was hung just below the water surface, and the chlorine was gradually released by osmosis. The method was uneconomic and too delicate to maintain. The next step was to use a hand pump (or mechanical pump) fitted on to a fully covered well mouth; this minimized the risks of pollution. Windmills are currently contemplated as a substitute for the expensive diesel engines, and efforts are being made to reduce the rather high capital costs of such a supply system.

(2)   Village latrines: The scheme was started in 1957. By 1968, there were 200,000 latrines in the State of Uttar Pradesh alone. The construction costs for one family are currently 10 US dollars. The project has included training programmes for masons, sanitary inspectors and village craftsmen, and a great effort was made to educate the villagers in the elementary principles of sanitation and hygiene.

198. International Bank for Reconstruction and Development/IDA, *Village Water Supply and Sanitation in Less Developed Countries.* (P.U. Report No. RES. 2., March 1974).

This report consists of a review of the current state of knowledge and of the experience of a large number of developing countries in the field of village water supply. It highlights the factors which are significant in determining the likelihood of success or failure of village water supply projects or programs, and there is a discussion of the problem of identifying and quantifying the benefits of investment in this field. Has an extensive bibliography.

199. International Bank for Reconstruction and Development/IDA, *Economic Evaluation of Public Utilities Projects.* P.U. Report No. GAS. 10., 1974).

Reviews the basic factors involved in the economic evaluation of water supply projects. While pointing out that the net benefits of investment should be maximized, the paper discusses the difficulties in quantifying the benefits of public utility projects. Cites two studies made by the Bank in Nairobi and Kuala Lumpur which aimed at estimating the benefits of water supply and sewerage projects by determining the impact of such investments on property values in the areas concerned. Similarly a survey of attempts to quantify the impact of improved water supplies on public health showed that statistically significant results were exceptionally difficult to obtain (despite large sample surveys) and were of little use in quantifying benefits. Problems arise not only in quantifying the economic and social benefits of an improvement in health, but also in disentangling the influence of improved sanitation facilities on health from all the many other influences such as nutrition, climate, and household income and assets.

200. International Development Research Council, *Technology Assessment and Research Priorities for Water Supply and Sanitation in Developing Countries: With special reference to rural populations and small communities.* (IDRC, Ottawa, Nov. 1973).

Emphasizes the development of low-cost technology with lower requirements for operation and maintenance than 'western' technology. It strongly calls into play local community or user-participation in project design and selection, in construction and in operation and maintenance. Recognizes the need for a flexible approach in rural communities which would involve finding out local perceptions, preferences and value systems; providing education on health consequences of improvements; and offering technical assistance to help in a series of incremental improvements to meet the aims of the users. Pages 125 to 128 discuss the difficulties of measuring the benefits accruing from improved water supplies and sanitation. Lists ten criteria for the development and selection of appropriate technologies, and provides an evaluation of existing and needed technologies in terms of these suggested criteria.

201. Lee T.R., *Residential Water Demand and Economic Development* (University of Toronto, Department of Geography, 1974).

Includes 13 case studies on water supply and public health in Calcutta. Emphasis is on the two extremes of the existing demand situation: (1) consumers in slums who are dependent on public water; and (2) consumers in good housing who have their own plumbing fixtures. Concludes that emphasis should be placed on meeting the existing unfilled demand. (i.e. on supplying the unserved population) rather than attempting to raise the level of supply to the whole population. Suggests that there will be a very strong possibility of overinvestment in water supply unless demand for water is given more importance in planning than in the past. A lower level of provision of water supply to all households will be more likely to lead to a higher level of total welfare than a high level of provision to a restricted section of the community.

202. Okun D.A., *Planning for Water Reuse* Development Digest Vol XI (3) July 1973.

Rapidly growing populations and increasing rates of urbanization and industrialization throughout the world are exerting greater pressures on limited water resources. This article suggests the development of a dual water system, that permits safe water reuse, as one method of coping with these demands. Pure water resources would be used for cooking, drinking, etc., while other water uses could be served from reclaimed waste-waters, polluted streams, or other waters of lesser quality. Gives examples of actual or planned reuse of waste water, and discusses the costs and benefits.

203. Okun D.A. and McJunkin F.E., *Common Sense in Community Water Supply* Development Digest Vol 5 (3) October 1967.

Points out that elaborate automatic equipment often makes little sense in countries where equally good results can be had through imaginative engineering and greater use of available labour. Gives examples of failures and problems of sophisticated water treatment plants, and cites several cases of more appropriate ways of dealing with water supplies and water disposal in developing countries. These include constant-flow valves in Zambia, water supply using bamboo pipes in Indonesia, a proportional chemical feeder using a paddle-wheel for dosing control in Swaziland, and large but simple alum-cake solution feeders in Santiago.

204. Parker R.N., 'The Introduction of Catchment Systems for Rural Water Supplies — A Benefit/Cost Study in a S.E. Ghana Village', *Agriculture in S.E. Ghana* (Ed) Dalton G.E. and Parker R.N. (Vol II. Development Study No. 13. Department of Agricultural Economics and Management, University of Reading, June 1973).

A case study of a typical S.E. Ghanaian village, located half a mile from a stream which serves as its main source of water. Suggests a range of water catchment systems suitable for both the individual householder and the community as a whole. All are based on the use of locally available materials, e.g. corrugated tin roofs for catchment areas, and concrete tanks for storage. Calculations are made of the time that is saved with such systems by the women who fetch the water, and is linked with the value of their time to produce benefit/cost ratios. These ratios can be used to compare investment in water catchment with that in other projects.

Concludes that small improvements to the individual household's water supply are highly beneficial, giving a benefit/cost ratio of up to 3.0 when 100 per cent of the time saved in collecting water is used for directly productive work, or up to 1.7 when 57 per cent of saved time is utilized. Constructing a community water supply which provides a regular amount of water throughout the year gives a benefit/cost ratio of between 1.3 and 2.3 (depending on the use to which time saved is put). However, if the systems do not attempt to provide a regular source of water, but seek to meet the community's needs for a short period only (usually during the peak demand for labour in cultivation), then the benefit/cost ratio rises significantly. For example, if 10 per cent of the water needs of the village are supplied by a catchment area such as a school roof, the benefit/cost ratio varies from 6.8 to 12.0.

205. Smith G., *Economics of Water Collection and Waste Recycling* (University of Cambridge, Department of Architecture, Autonomous Housing Study, Working Paper No. 6., July 1973).

A report on the economics of waste treatment and water supply for domestic premises not connected to mains servicing. Waste treatment by aerobic and anaerobic biological stabilization is discussed, along with water supply from rainwater collection with some recycling. Concludes that the costs of such servicing is roughly twice as much as that of mains-servicing at low density. However, further research is proceeding to devise a more economical system. Includes an appendix on anaerobic digestion with methane production from primary vegetable wastes.

206. Stern P.H., *Low Cost Development of Water Resources* Paper presented at the University of Edinburgh Appropriate Technology Conference, September, 1973.

Covers the use of polythene for the construction of low-cost small-scale rainwater catchments, and the role of bamboo and plastics in reducing the cost of piping water. Gives comparative costs of using metal and plastic pipes in dollars per linear foot in 1967:

Use and size	Copper	Galvanized Steel	Polythene	PVC
Interior supply				
½"	0.26	0.18	0.05	0.11
1"	0.62	0.33	0.15	0.17
2"	1.72	0.72	0.60	0.45
Drain, waste, vent				
2½"	1.23	1.08	0.69	0.65
4"	2.55	2.16		1.60

207. White G.F., Bradley D.J., and White A.U., *Drawers of Water: Domestic Water Use in East Africa* (Chicago, 1972).

Water supply improvements in the developing world have not kept up with population growth, especially in urban areas. To achieve maximum benefit from the expenditures made to remedy this gap, water projects must be based on greater knowledge of how water is used in the community, and how water improvements affect economic growth and community development and health. The conclusion drawn from this case study in East Africa is that, with both supply and disposal of water, once a minimum service is provided, the unit gain to health from units of improvement probably decreases sharply. Preliminary evidence suggests that slow development of ideal 'Western type' water systems should be set aside in favour of more rapid delivery of smaller quantities of potable water to every household.

C. Health

208. Abel-Smith B., *Health Priorities in Developing Countries: The Economist's Contribution,* International Journal of Health Services Vol 2 (1) 1972.

Argues that the greatest contribution which the economist can make to health planning is not in the development of models, but in cost-effectiveness studies. The value of such studies is illustrated by an example — the study of the expansion of medical education in developing countries, which could contribute substantially less to health than if the resources were used in alternative ways.

209 Abel-Smith B., *Cost-effectiveness and Cost-Benefit in Cholera Control* WHO Chronicle Vol 27, 1973.

Explains how economic principles can be applied to the calculation of the total cost of a disease such as cholera. A cost/benefit analysis comparing the benefits of a treatment-only approach with the benefits of a treatment plus vaccination, or a treatment plus sanitation approach, could lead to a greater rationalization of investment in the health sector.

210. Biddulph J., *Report on a Brief Visit to the People's Republic of China.* 1973.

Reports on medical achievements in China, and the Chinese medical system in urban and rural areas. Comments that the Chinese spend one tenth as much per capita on health as the Government of Papua New Guinea, and yet achieve more. Acknowledges that socio-economic, political, and cultural factors are involved. However, some aspects of the Chinese system are probably fairly easily adaptable for use in other developing countries.

211. Cohn E.J., *Assessing the Costs and Benefits of Anti-Malaria Programmes: The Indian Experience* American Journal of Public Health, March 1973.

Compares the costs and benefits of controlling versus eradicating malaria. Evaluations made using different discount rates gave the following results:

Present Value (1957/8) of Control Programme versus
Eradication Programme over a 30 year period. (Crores Rs.)

Discount rate (%)	Control	Eradication
6	83.5	65.4
8	68.5	61.3
10	57.2	57.4
12	49.0	54.2
14	42.5	50.8

Shows that up to a discount rate of 10 per cent, control of malaria is the preferred technique. Eradication would be preferred at higher discount rates.

212. Dorozynski A., *Doctors and Healers* (Ottawa, International Development Research Council, 1975). IDRC — 043e.

Developing countries, in their desire to 'catch up' with richer ones, have emulated the models of modern medicine. This booklet asks whether governments can afford this approach, and, even if they could, would this be the most effective and least disruptive way of providing health care? It argues for innovative approaches to assure that adequate basic health services are easily available to everyone, at a price that everyone can afford. A few of the new approaches being initiated are described. The major case studies are of (1) barefoot doctors in China; (2) lay-healers in Guatemala; and (3) medical auxiliaries in Iran. Also quotes studies which reveal that, after a few weeks of training, healers can make a proper diagnosis, and prescribe appropriate treatment in at least 70 per cent of all cases.

213. Elliot K., *Using Medical Auxiliaries: Some Ideas and Examples* Contact (Christian Medical Commission, World Council of Churches, October 1972.)

Gives examples of existing schemes for training and using medical auxiliaries in the U.S.A., the U.K., and the U.S.S.R., Fiji, Africa, and the People's Republic of China. Includes some cost comparisons. For example, in Kenya it cost £1,000 to train an auxiliary, as opposed to £10,000 for a medical graduate. In Uganda, 3 years of training for an assistant cost £500, as opposed to £10,000 for a graduate.

214. Gish O., *The Way Forward*, World Health April 1975.

Examines health strategies in Tanzania. Hospital expansion is no longer a priority, with emphasis being given instead to the provision of basic health services to all citizens through rural health centres. Estimates that the capital cost of a small dispensary is 7,000 dollars, with an annual operating cost of 4,000 dollars. A rural health centre would have capital costs amounting to 75,000 dollars, with annual operating costs of 25,000 dollars. These estimates compare very favourably with the cost of providing hospital beds; the *per bed* capital costs of a new hospital range from 4,000 to 25,000 dollars, while the annual operating costs *per bed* range from 1,000 to 4,000 dollars. It is hoped to provide one dispensary for every 6,500 people by 1980, and to provide one rural health centre for every 50,000 people. As the following table shows, the change in emphasis from hospitals to health centres has been matched by a change in emphasis from graduate doctors to medical assistants or auxiliaries:

	Graduate doctors	Assistant Medical officers	Medical assistants	Rural Medical aides
1961 (number)	403	22	200	380
1980 (planned)	800	300	1,200	2,800

215. Mosley W.H., Bart K.J., and Sommer A., *An Epidemiological Assessment of Cholera Control Programs in Rural East Pakistan,* International Journal of Epidemiology 1972.

Compares immunization programs with the establishment of treatment centres for dealing with cases of cholera (i.e. pre-care versus post-care). Finds little difference in the costs of the two techniques, but the treatment centres are almost 100 per cent effective, while the immunization programme has very low efficiency and is of very little practical public health value. Concludes that ultimate control and eradication will come only when a satisfactory vaccine has been developed, or when modern concepts and methods of sanitation can be universally applied in rural areas.

216. National Academy of Sciences, *Mosquito Control: Some Perspectives for Developing Countries.* (N.A.S., Washington, 1973).

Examines some biological-control alternatives to conventional pesticides, and evaluates the potential of these various approaches.

217. Rifkin S., and Kaplinsky R., *Health Strategy and Development Planning. Lessons from the People's Republic of China.* (Sussex, Science Policy Research Unit, mimeo, 1974).

Includes a discussion on how to evaluate health and medical care services in developing countries. Evaluates the Chinese health system within the framework of a cost/benefit analysis. Points out the difficulty in identifying all the costs and benefits of health services, but reaches the general conclusion that health policies in China are appropriate to the country's factor proportions and health needs. Considers that although it would appear *a priori* that the Chinese system could profitably be transferred to other developing countries, a number of factors must be considered in this transfer. In particular, health policies should first be integrated into overall development plans. Specific aspects of the Chinese policy might then be considered e.g. great stress on prevention, use of health teams and auxiliaries, and decentralization of services. Useful bibliography.

218. Speight A.N.P. *Cost-effectiveness and Drug Therapy,* Tropical Doctor April 1975.

Explains that expensive drugs are often prescribed in developing countries when a much cheaper and equally effective alternative is available. This is thought to be due to such factors as the influence of advertising, bias towards expensive drugs in teaching hospitals, etc. Suggests that it is desirable for developing countries to develop their own pharmaceutical industries for the production of 'low-cost' drugs. Such an industry would serve the country's needs, generate employment, and save foreign exchange currently used on the importation of 'inappropriate' expensive drugs.

219. Wheeler M., *The Economics of the Medical Auxiliary,* Paper presented at the University of East Africa Social Science Council Conference. (Makere, Kampala, Dec. 1969).

Examines the economic case for the employment of medical auxiliaries in developing countries, in preference to persons with professional qualifications. Claims that the decision is whether to bias investment in favour of auxiliaries, or in favour of professionals. That is, both are needed, but in what ratio? Claims that it is impossible to evaluate economic benefits, but shows how a comparison of costs can be made using discounting procedures. Using figures from Kenya, shows that, depending on the discount rate used, 1.97 to 2.88 auxiliaries could have been employed for every professional forgone.

Administrators must then decide whether benefits from a professional are at least twice as great as those from an auxiliary. If not, then additional investment should be in auxiliaries. Concludes that had such a method as this been applied to the appraisal of medical manpower decisions over the last few years, very different decisions would have emerged.

220. World Health June 1972 (W.H.O.) Special issue on medical auxiliaries.

Case studies of medical assistants in Ethiopia, medical auxiliaries in Algeria and Central African Republic, 'feldshers' in the USSR, and physician assistants in the USA.

D. Roads and Transport Technology

221. Bourke W.O., *Basic Vehicle for South East Asia,* Technology and Economics in Economic Development (USAID, May 1972).

Describes the development of an intermediate vehicle — the Fiera — by Ford. The vehicle is more efficient than the traditional animal or human-powered vehicles, and less expensive than imported vehicles (thus reaching a much larger proportion of the population of South East Asia). It consists of a simple cab and chassis, but variations are possible so that it can be used as a truck, a passenger bus, or a van, and it can be used to drive a rice-husking machine, power a water pump or a saw. Construction is labour-intensive and use is made of locally available materials, labour and skills.

222. Cabanos P., *Jeepney Manufacturing in the Philippines: A Model for Developing the Agricultural Machinery Industry,* Agricultural Mechanization in Asia, Autumn 1971.

Describes how the 'jeepney' industry started in the Philippines after World War II, based on a preponderance of cheap surplus material and a great need for public conveyance. The jeepney is a low cost, simple vehicle based on a re-conditioned engine (in 1971, a jeepney capable of carrying 12 persons cost 1,600 dollars). As soon as the concept was developed, small shops producing crude versions cropped up almost overnight, and the industry has flourished to such an extent that annual sales in 1971 had reached 17 million dollars. Gives details of two large companies which started from scratch in the 1950's using simple tools.

223.. Howe J., *Surface Transport in Africa — the Future,* Journal of the Royal Society of Arts, August 1975.

Argues for a move towards low-standard high-density road networks. Suggests that this might favour the greater use of labour-intensive methods of construction. A greater emphasis on local roads ought to be accompanied by a re-assessment of local vehicle needs. In this respect, the author looks at various appropriate adaptations of bicycles and motorcycles.

224. International Bank for Reconstruction and Development/IDA, *Study of the Substitution of Labour for Equipment in Road Construction* (mimeo, October, 1971).

Looks at the increase in economic costs required to employ successively more labour in road construction to the point of displacing virtually all equipment for the sake of job creation. Concludes that it is technically feasible to substitute labour for equipment in all but 10 to 20 per cent of total construction costs, and for all but 2 to 15 per cent of costs if an 'intermediate' quality is acceptable. However, economic feasibility of using more labour-intensive methods will depend on the productivity of labour and machines, and on the prevailing wage rate for labour. Concludes that intermediate technologies combining capital-intensive and labour-intensive methods appear promising and should be further investigated.

225. International Labour Office, *Employment, Incomes and Equality: A strategy for increasing productive employment in Kenya.* (ILO, Geneva, 1972). Technical Paper No. 8: Employment and Technical Choice in Road Construction.

A case study which shows the dangers of persisting in 'extremes' in road building. A straightforward comparison between a labour-intensive method of building a gravel road, and a capital-intensive method, showed that the latter would be the cheaper, even if a shadow wage rate was used. However, when the choice of methods was increased to five, by considering various combinations of the original two 'extremes', the more labour-intensive of the 'mixed' methods was found to be the cheapest.

226. Irvin G., *Roads and Redistribution: Social Costs and Benefits of Labour Intensive Road Construction in Iran* (ILO, Geneva, 1975).

Investigates to what extent the substitution of more labour for some of the machinery used in road building in Iran would be justified in social terms. Analysis is based on detailed case studies of one highway, two feeder roads, and two rural roads. Concludes that although the adoption of more labour-intensive techniques is uneconomic from the point of view of the private entrepreneur, these techniques would be socially feasible for each of the roads examined. Whether or not it is socially desirable depends on the priorities the Government attaches to maintaining a high rate of future income, as against reducing present inequalities, particularly as between the urban and rural sectors. The payment of a subsidy to contractors willing to employ more labour is suggested as the most practical and direct means of altering the capital/labour ratio.

227. Lal D., *Men or Machines: A Philippine Case Study of Labour/Capital Substitution in Road Construction.* (ILO, Geneva, forthcoming).

Compares labour-intensive methods with capital-intensive methods for the construction of gravel-surfaced roads, and concrete-paved roads. Findings are summarized in the table:

	Gravel-road		Concrete-slab	
	Labour Intensive	Capital Intensive	Labour Intensive	Capital Intensive
	(pesos per Km).		(pesos per 1000m^3)	
Market prices	123,700	136,600	2,153	2,137
Shadow prices:				
High shadow wage/low rental rate	100,700	112,000	1,725	1,504
Low shadow wage/high rental rate	87,500	144,300	1,709	1,737

For gravel roads, the labour-intensive method compares very favourably at both market and shadow prices. With concrete slabs, however, the labour-intensive method is preferable only when a low shadow wage and a high shadow rate for renting equipment are assumed. It is estimated that if the labour-intensive methods are used throughout, 70 to 100 per cent more jobs would be created than if the capital-intensive methods were used.

228. Muller J., *Labour-Intensive Methods in Low-Cost Road Construction: A Case Study,* International Labour Review Vol 101 (1) Jan/June 1970.

Case study of a project in sub-tropical Africa which started out as a highly mechanized project but had to resort to increasingly labour-intensive methods. The higher indirect operational costs of the capital-intensive method, and the associated economic cost of delays in opening the road narrowed its cost advantage over the most labour-intensive method. The author suggests that if shadow prices were used and the social benefits of employment considered, the labour-intensive method would have been best. A mixed strategy is advocated, using more mechanized techniques for certain processes.

See also **Muller J.**, *Choice of Technology in Underdeveloped Countries, Exemplified by Road Construction in East Africa.* (The Technical University of Denmark, 1973).

229. Schlie T.W., *Appropriate Technology: Some concepts, some ideas, and some recent experiences in Africa,* East African Journal of Rural Development. Vol. 7 (1&2) 1974.

Cites the building of the Tan-Zam Railway as an important example of technological choice. This particular aid project was turned down by USAID, IBRD, UK, etc. on economic grounds, while the Chinese, presumably using different evaluation techniques, found the project to be viable. The railway has been built using highly labour-intensive methods: it is estimated that 80,000 Chinese and 80,000 Tanzanian labourers have been employed in the project. The author asks how the Americans would have built the railway.

230. SIET Institute, *Appropriate Technology for Indian Industry.* (Hyderabad, 1964).

Includes a case study comparing a hand-operated and a power-driven technique for manufacturing a cycle gear-case. At a level of production of 3,000 cases per month, the hand method was found to be cheaper, and generated a larger surplus:

	Hand-operated	Power-driven
Capital equipment (Rs)	35,200	80,000
Total employees	27	18
Cost per unit (Rs)	5.66	5.77

231. United Nations Industrial Development Organization, *Bicycles: A Case Study of Indian Experience* (Small-scale Manufacturing Studies. No. 1. U.N., New York, 1969).

Compares production data for firms in the small-scale and in the large-scale sectors in 1966, and gives detailed figures of production costs for plants producing 25,000 and 15,000 bicycles per annum. Concludes that because of recent technological innovations and lower overheads, certain components can be produced more cheaply by the small-scale sector.

Section 5

Handbooks, Manuals, Buyers' Guides and Technical Publications

---

232. Alley R., *Travels in China 1966-1971.* (New World Press, Peking, 1973). Gives details of ferro-cement boat construction, a simple mechanized rice transplanter, an electric winch for cable cultivation, simple well-sinking techniques, bridge building and irrigation works.

233. American Peace Corps., *Wells Manual for Volunteers* (APC., Upper Volta, 1970). Provides information on a wide range of well construction techniques used in Africa.

234. American Peace Corps., *Poultry Booklet* (APC., New Delhi, 1970). A simple guide, based on experience in India, for individuals in developing countries interested in a commercial poultry enterprise.

235. *Appropriate Technology.* Quarterly journal, Intermediate Technology Publications, London. A forum for the exchange of ideas among those directly involved in development work. Useful technical articles include:

   (a) *Agricultural Equipment:* foot-powered thresher Vol 2(2); simple manual maize shelling device Vol 2(1); new agricultural machines from the International Rice Research Institute Vol 2(1); tie-ridgers in Zambia Vol 1(3); pit silos in South Chad Vol 1(3).

   (b) *Water Supplies:* Pitcher farming Vol 1(3); Nepalese Water Mill Vol 1(3); Water pipes from bamboo Vol 1(2); the Humphrey Pump Vol 2(1).

   (c) *Low cost housing and building materials:* Low cost housing in Ghana Vol 1(1), in Kerala Vol 1(1), in India Vol 1(3), and in the Pacific Islands Vol 1(2); Indigenous building methods Vol 2(2); wood preservation in developing countries Vol 2(2); brick manufacture Vol 2(1); lime and surkhi manufacture Vol 1(4).

   (d) *Energy:* Methane Vol 1(1) and Vol 2(2); solar water heaters Vol 1(3); solar steam cookers Vol 1(2).

   (e) *Roads and Transport:* Low cost roads Vol 1(2); wheelbarrows Vol 2(2); cycle rickshaws Vol 1(2); medium-span wooden bridge in Kenya Vol 1(4).

   (f) *Miscellaneous:* Low-cost refrigerated incubator Vol 1(1); intermediate food technology Vol 1(1); village aluminium project Vol 1(1); ferrocement boatbuilding Vol 2(1); a cheap incinerator Vol 2(1).

236. **Bell C. et al.,** *Methane: fuel of the future.* (Prism Press, Dorchester, 1975). Describes the process of methane generation; looks at current uses of methane, current research and developments; and the potential of methane in meeting future energy needs.

237. **Bharadwaj R.S. et al.,** *Manual for Fish Culture in Rajasthan and Madhya Pradesh.* (APC., New Delhi, 1973). Prepared for the private farmer interested in raising fish, and for panchayats who wish to utilize their village ponds more profitably. Covers stocking, breeding, fish diseases, equipment, harvesting and transport.

238. **Cecoco,** *Guide book for Rural Cottage and Small and Medium Scale Industries: Paddy Rice Cultivation.* (Cecoco, Japan, 1972). A comprehensive guide published by the Cecoco company covering a wide range of their small-scale machinery for manufacturing and agricultural production.

239. **Dancy H.K.,** *Manual on Building Construction.* (Intermediate Technology Publications, London, 1973). A practical illustrated handbook on construction of small buildings using local materials, suitable for a great variety of ground and climatic conditions.

240. **Department of Housing and Urban Development, Office of International Affairs, Washington,** *Handbook for Building Homes of Earth,* 1975. Takes the newest techniques developed in modern soil mechanics and puts them into simple terms so that almost anyone, anywhere, can have the benefit of the great amount of work that has been done by the scientists.

241. **Food and Agriculture Organization,** *Equipment Related to the Domestic Functions of Food Preparation, Handling and Storage.* (FAO, Rome, 1974). A kit of information and instructional aids for rural development programmes, prepared for the use of educators and extensionists in rural development.

242. **Food and Agriculture Organization,** *Equipment and Methods for Improved Smoke-drying of Fish* (FAO, Rome, 1971). Fisheries Technical Paper No.104.

243. **Forest Products Research Centre,** *Manual of Rural Wood Preservation* (Department of Forests, Papua New Guinea, 1974). Describes methods of making traditional building materials such as bamboo, timber and poles more durable.

244. **Fry L.J. and Merill R.,** *Methane Digesters: For Fuel gas and Fertilizer.* (L.J. Fry, California, 1973). A valuable treatment of methane systems and research. Includes designs for a small and an intermediate scale system.

245. **Fry L.J.,** *Practical Building of Methane Power Plants.* (D.A. Knox, Andover, 1974).

246. **Intermediate Technology Development Group,** *The Introduction of Rain-water Catchment Tanks and Micro-Irrigation in Botswana.* (Intermediate Technology Publications, London, 1969). Report of a field project.

247. **ITDG,** *Chemicals from Biological Resources.* (Intermediate Technology Publications, London; 1973). A survey of chemicals obtainable by simple processes from renewable natural resources. Now out of print but revised edition forthcoming.

248. **ITDG,** *Guide to Hand-operated and Animal-drawn Equipment.* Intermediate Technology Publications, London, 1973). Gives details and lists of manufacturers on a wide range of low-cost farming and food processing implements in UK and abroad. Revised and expanded edition forthcoming.

249. **ITDG,** *How to make a Metal-Bending Machine.* (Intermediate Technology Publications, London, 1973).

250. **ITDG,** *Methane Production of Anaerobic Fermentation.* (Intermediate Technology Publications, London, 1975). Proceedings of a recent ITDG seminar on methane.

251. **ITDG,** *Oil Drum Forges.* (Intermediate Technology Publications, London, 1975). Specifications for making a simple forge from an oil drum with (a) foot-operated bellows pump; and (b) hand-operated fan.

252. **ITDG,** *The Iron Foundry — An Industrial Profile.* (Intermediate Technology Publications, London, 1975). The first of a series designed to provide information on production equipment and costings for different areas of industrial technology. Also included are fuels, labour requirements, and a bibliography useful to anyone starting small-scale foundry work.

253. **Krusch P.,** *Poultry Handbook for Africa.* (APC., Sierra Leone, 1970). Covers housing, feeding and watering of chickens; brooding, growing and laying periods; and handling and marketing of eggs.

254. **Lock C.,** *Some Notes and Suggestions on Hand-Milling and Making Hand-Mills.* (ITDG, mimeo, undated). Written for people interested in the problems of hand-milling grain. Outlines the problems, provides information on equipment available for milling, and illustrates hand-mills which, with some modifications, could be manufactured in villages.

255. **MacKillop A.,** *Why Soft Technology? Alternative Solutions to the Energy Crisis.* (Methuen, London, 1975). Discusses the philosophy of soft technology and examines the potential of windpower, solar energy, methane and small-scale hydropower for meeting future energy needs for agriculture industry, domestic heating, lighting and cooking, and transport. Useful references to research organizations working on soft technology. Short bibliography.

256. **Maddocks D.,** *Report on Low-Cost Waterproof Membranes.* (Intermediate Technology Publications, London, 1975). Presents the basic methods of construction of membranes to be used to line rainwater catchment areas or water storages. Includes sample costing and a bibliography.

257. **Mann H.T. and Williamson D.,** *Water Treatment and Sanitation* (Intermediate Technology Publications, London. Revised edition 1976). A handbook of simple methods for rural areas in developing countries.

258. **Minimum Cost Housing Group,** *Stop the Five Gallon Flush* (McGill University, School of Architecture, 1973). A comprehensive survey of alternative waste disposal systems. Concerned mainly with low-cost technologies and systems which are self-contained and use little or no water.

259. **Portola Institute,** *Energy Primer: Solar, Water, Wind and Bio-fuels.* (Portola Institute, 1974). A comprehensive technical book about renewable forms of energy. Each section includes a detailed series of book and publication reviews as a guide to further reading, and there is a comprehensive listing of organizations and manufacturers offering appropriate equipment and services.

260. **Ressler E.,** *Considerations for the Use of Wind Power for Borehole Pumping* (Appropriate Technology Unit, Ethiopia, Christian Relief and Development Association, Report No. 1., 1975). Attempts to outline broad conditions useful for those interested in using wind power for borehole pumping. Includes a brief introduction to windmill design; wind requirements and wind data collection; site selection; and a brief description of some structural components.

261. **Rogers J.F. et. al.,** *An Illustrated Guide to Fish Preparation.* (Tropical Products Institute Report No. G.83., 1975). A guide covering equipment, hygiene and methods of preparing various types of fish. Intended primarily for training purposes in developing countries.

262. **Sherman M.M.,** *6,000 Hand-Crafted Sailing Windmills of Lassithiou, Greece, and their Relevance to Windmill Development in Rural India.* Paper presented at the International Conference on Appropriate Technologies for Semiarid Areas: Wind and Solar Energy for Water Supply, (Berlin, September, 1975). Ascertains the reasons for the widespread use of windmills in Crete, and determines if any of the details of their design could be incorporated in the design of water pumping windmills currently being developed for widespread use in rural India.

263. **Sherman M.M.,** *An Interim Report: The Design and Construction of an Appropriate Water Pumping Windmill for Agriculture in India.* Paper presented at the International Conference on Appropriate Technologies for Semiarid Areas: Wind and Solar Energy for Water Supply, (Berlin, September,

1975). Looks at the development of windmills to pump water as an alternative to diesel oil pumps and bullock operated pumps.

264. **United Nations, Department of Social and Economic Affairs,** *Manual on Self-Help Housing.* (U.N., New York, 1964). Intended for the use of government services and private agencies that are considering low-cost, self-help housing programs. It states in technical and administrative terms the principles and techniques that have been evolved from an evaluation of many projects throughout the world.

265. **Volunteers In Technical Assistance, Inc.,** *Village Technology Handbook.* (VITA, New York, 1970). Contains a variety of low-cost technological innovations collected from rural volunteers to be useful to future volunteers.

266. **Watt S.B.,** *A Manual on the Automatic Hydraulic Ram Pump.* (Intermediate Technology Publications, London, 1975). Contains details of how to make and maintain a small hydraulic ram on a suitable site.

267. *World Crops* Vol 20(2) April 1968: Supplement 'Equipment and services for tropical agriculture'. A guide to equipment designed specifically for use in tropical or sub-tropical farming.

268. *World Crops* Vol 27(5) 1975. 'Tropical crop processing and drying and storage equipment'. A guide to machines, driers and silos available for use in hot climates.

Section 6

Some Relevant Bibliographies

269. **Akhtar S.,** *Health Care in the People's Republic of China: A bibliography with abstracts.* (International Development Research Council, Ottawa, 1975). IDRC — 038e.

270. **Akhtar S.,** *Low-cost rural health care and health manpower training.* (IDRC, Ottawa, 1975). IDRC — 042e.

271. **Baranson J.,** *Technology for Underdeveloped Areas: An Annotated Bibliography.* (Pergamon Press, 1967).

272. **Bateman G.H.,** *A Bibliography of Low-Cost Water Technologies.* (Intermediate Technology Publications, London, 1974). 3rd edition.

273. **Bell C. and Amarshi A.,** *Agricultural Mechanization in Asia and Africa: An Annotated Bibliography.* (ODA/IDS, London, 1973).

274. **Brace Research Institute,** *Annual Report 1974,* pp 34-39. List of Publications. (Brace Research Institute, MacGill University, 1974).

275. **Brode J.,** *The Process of Modernization: An Annotated Bibliography on the Sociocultural Aspects of Development.* (Harvard University Press, 1969).

276. **Dean G.C.,** *Technological Innovation in Chinese Industry.* (Mansell, London, 1972).

277. **Dejene T. and Smith S.E.,** *Experiences in Rural Development: A selected annotated bibliography of planning, implementing and evaluating rural development in Africa.* (American Council on Education, Washington, 1973). OLC Paper No. 1.

278. **Dendy D.A.V.,** *Composite Flour Technology: A bibliography.* (Tropical Products Institute Report No. G.89, 1975).

279. **Elliott K.,** *The Training of Auxiliaries in Health Care: An Annotated Bibliography.* (Intermediate Technology Publications, London, 1975).

280. **Harper P.,** *Directory of Alternative Technology.* Published in three parts in Architectural Design — Vol XLIV (11) 1974; Vol XLV (4) 1975; and Vol XLV (5) 1975.

281. Ganiere N., *Transfer of Technology and Appropriate Techniques: A Bibliography.* (OECD, Development Centre, Paris, 1973).

282. Ganiere N., *The Process of Industrialization of China: Primary Elements of an Analytical Bibliography.* (OECD, Development Centre, Paris, 1974).

283. **International Development Research Council.,** *List of Publications for 1970-73.* (IDRC, Ottawa, 1974). IDRC – 030e.

284. Jackson S., *Economically Appropriate Technologies for Developing Countries: A Survey.* (Overseas Development Council, Occasional Paper No.3., Washington, 1972).

285. Jenkins G., *Non-Agricultural Choice of Technique: An Annotated Bibliography of Empirical Studies* (Institute of Commonwealth Studies, Oxford, 1975).

286. Manning D., *Disaster Technology: An Annotated Bibliography.* (Pergamon Press, 1974).

287. **Massey Ferguson (Toronto) Ltd.,** *The Pace and Form of Farm Mechanization in the Developing Countries.* (Massey Ferguson, 1974).

288. Schofield S., *Village Nutrition Studies: An Annotated Bibliography.* (Institute of Development Studies, University of Sussex, 1975).

289. Slate F., *Low-cost Housing for Developing Countries: An Annotated Bibliography 1950-1972.* (Cornell University, 1974).

290. **Tropical Products Institute,** *Publications List.* 1975.

291. White A.U. and Seviour C., *Rural Water Supply and Sanitation in Less Developed Countries: A Selected Annotated Bibliography.* (IDRC, Ottawa, 1974).

Authors Index

96

Country Index

Subject Index